ALSO BY JESSICA B. HARRIS

HOT STUFF: A COOKBOOK IN
PRAISE OF THE PIQUANT

IRON POTS AND WOODEN SPOONS:
AFRICA'S GIFTS TO NEW WORLD COOKING

TRADITIONAL CARIBBEAN COOKING

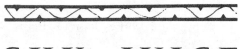

SKY JUICE

AND

FLYING

FISH

JESSICA B. HARRIS

A FIRESIDE BOOK PUBLISHED BY
SIMON & SCHUSTER
NEW YORK   LONDON   TORONTO
SYDNEY   TOKYO   SINGAPORE

FIRESIDE
Simon & Schuster Building
Rockefeller Center
1230 Avenue of the Americas
New York, New York 10020

FIRESIDE and colophon are registered trademarks
of Simon & Schuster

Designed by Bonni Leon
Manufactured in the United States of America

7   9   10   8

Library of Congress Cataloging in Publication Data

Harris, Jessica B.
Sky juice and flying fish: / traditional Caribbean cooking / Jessica Harris.
p.   cm.
"A Fireside book."
Includes index.
1. Cookery, Caribbean.   I. Title.
TX716.A1H374   1991
641.59729—dc20   90-48012
CIP

ISBN 0-671-68165-6

"Creole Feast: An Island-by-Island Look at Caribbean Cooking" originally appeared in slightly different form in an advertising supplement
entitled "Creole Feast: The Culinary Caribbean," in the April 3, 1989,
issue of *The New Yorker*.

To my mother, Rhoda A. Harris, and the memory
of my father, Jesse B. Harris (ibae), who dressed
me in gold and gave me the world

To my Caribbean sisters, June Bobb (Guyana),
Carol Cadogan (Barbados), Michèle Marcelin
(Haiti), Marcella Martinez (New York), Patricia
Lawrence (New York), Maryse Pochot
(Guadeloupe), and Maria Williams (Jamaica), who
assure me that my not being from the region is
simply an accident of passport

And to the memory of relatives and friends who
have gone on leaving the taste of rum, coconuts,
and chile on my tongue

ACKNOWLEDGMENTS

No one can create a cookbook without relying on those who came before. So I must first acknowledge a debt to all of those known and unknown Caribbean grannies, *gran'meres, abuelitas,* and *welas* who have left us their culinary legacy.

Then, I want to thank all of those who enabled me to take this Caribbean odyssey: Myron Clement and Joe Petrocik of Clement Petrocik; Cécile Graffin of the French West Indies Tourist Office; Markly Wilson of the Caribbean Tourism Organization; Meridith Pilon and Nora Broussard of the Rowland Company; Jacques Guannel and Muriel Wiltord of the Martinique Tourist Office; Erick W. Rotin and Guy Claude Germain of the Guadeloupe Tourist Office; Karen Weiner Escalera and Marilyn Marx of Karen Weiner Escalera Associates; Maryse Chancy of the Haiti Hotel Association; Linda Kundell of Herman Associates; Peter Rotholz of Peter Rotholz Associates; Joe Scott and Tony Tedeschi of Scott Tedeschi; Patricia Nehaul of the Barbados Board of Tourism; Joan Bloom of Hill and Knowlton and the Saint Lucia Tourist Board; Lou Hammond of Lou Hammond Associates; Dinaz Boga of Jensen Boga; Joan Medhurst of Medhurst and Associates; Leona Bryant of the U.S.V.I. Division of Tourism; Abraham Pokrassa and Fina Soto of the Curacao Tourist Office; Margaret Zellers, Barbara Gillam, and the M and Ms at Marcella Martinez Associates.

My international Caribbean family, who fed me, let me into their kitchens, and put up with my questions, must also be thanked. Stella St.-John in Barbados; J. Irving Pearman, Gary Phillips, and Regina Fleming in Bermuda; Nelly and family in the Dominican Republic; "Mama" and Betty Mascoll in Grenada; Carmelita Jeanne (Maman Guadeloupe), Jennifer and Bruce Pochot, Simone and André Schwarz-Bart, and Gérard, Marie-Claude, and Liaura Virginius in Guadeloupe; Beryl and Preston Bobb in Guyana; Roger Dunwell, Adrienne and Michel-Ange Voltaire, Max Beauvoir and Antonio Fénélon in Haiti; Averile Bodden, Norma Shirley, Larry Bailey and Asif Williams in Jamaica; Uncle Greg and Aunt Mona Jones, and the folks at Bacardi in Puerto Rico; Candy Montano and family in Trinidad and Tobago; Janet Foster, Margaret Mroz and family, Jan Gernon and Leona Watson in the U.S. Virgin Islands; Cecily Rodway, Ron Phillips, Joseph, Sybil, and Karen Clarke in New York.

Thanks also to the numerous librarians, culinary historians, and well wishers who shared information and helped schedule: Mary Hanratty, Nancy Harmon Jenkins, Mabel McCarthy, Maricel Persilla, Ruth Warantz, and all those at the reference desk at the national library in Kingston, Jamaica.

A particular thanks goes to those who came, ate, and commented: Richard Alleman, Kamau Bobb, Lurita Brown, Cynthia Bunton, Linda Cohen, Lynne and Pat Eck, Ayoluwa Fenner, Karen Kopta, Yvette Burgess Polcyn, and Felami, and Cheikh Oumar Thiam.

A large "Whew!" with thanks for my editor, Sydny Miner, and my agent, Carole Abel, who got *Sky Juice and Flying Fish* from the beach to the kitchen and into the bookstores.

Finally, a thanks to my mother, Rhoda, for always being there.

CONTENTS

INTRODUCTION

For many people, the Caribbean region means sun, sand, and sea. Matters culinary, if thought of at all, are a reference to "ackee, rice, saltfish are nice/ and the rum is fine any time of year," or the Yellowbird and Rum Bamboozle cocktails at the manager's cocktail party. For all too many, food in the Caribbean is made up of insipid hotel dining with toned-down local specialties and continental cuisine, or a stop at a beach bar for a bad hamburger. This situation doesn't have to be.

For the adventurous, the Caribbean region provides vast opportunities for culinary explorations. Eat with the folk in small restaurants where foods are lovingly prepared by local chefs. Check out the roadside stands or amble into one of the many rum shacks for a chat with the resident "bar association." In these places, seafood, fried, stewed, or boiled, is usually the order of the day accompanied by a starch or a bread. Helpings are copious and there is no extra charge for the friends you'll make and the local lore you'll pick up. Each island has its own variations on the regional cuisine.

In the small restaurants where it is possible to sample local fare, decor usually leans heavily toward brightly colored floral plastic tablecloths, which are topped with Woolworth's bud vases filled with bougainvillea and hibiscus and an astonishing array of pepper sauces. Don't let the decor fool you; some of the best food in the region is available in these humble-looking spots. You might enjoy delights ranging from a perfect chicken creole, like the one that I tasted at Chez Mak on the French side of Saint Martin, or the stewed fish and funghi that I sampled in what seemed to be a transplanted version of the same restaurant in French Town in Saint Thomas, or the fried fish and bammie that I gobbled down in a waterfront restaurant in Port Royal, Jamaica.

Road food is not for the timid or cholesterol-conscious. Stop for *chicharrón* in Bayamón, Puerto Rico. These are George Bush's pork rinds prepared by heavenly hands. Indeed pork may be a roadside leitmotif in the Caribbean. Nibble spicy jerked pork at a pork pit in Jamaica or sample succulent chicharrón de cerdo con yuca in the Dominican Republic. For a change of pace, pull over and simply have a taste of coconut water. This delicate liquid is ambrosial when sampled roadside under a palm-fringed sky. Don't miss the Sno-Cones prepared with tropical syrups such as passion fruit, sapodilla, and mango. Each island has its own variation and its own name for this refreshing sweet: Sky Juice in Jamaica, *Piraguas* in

Puerto Rico, *Frio Frios* in the Dominican Republic, *Frescos* in Haiti, and *Snobols* in Guadeloupe.

Language is part of the difficulty with some of the food of the Caribbean: What root is what? and what do you call this here? are two constant questions. But language is also part of the fun—and Caribbean food is fun. The humor of the islands is vividly expressed in its foods. Where else could you taste a dish called Run Down, because you put it in the pot and cook it until it "runs down." Perhaps you want to try Dip and Fall Back, a Caribbean cousin of fondue. In Cuba, you can savor a dish of black beans and white rice called the Christians and the Moors, while in Guadeloupe feel the heat of a chile called Madame Jacques' behind. (I've always wondered who Madame Jacques was.)

Confectionery gets into the act too. At the ferry slip on Ile des Saintes, you'll be greeted by vendors selling tourment d'amour (love's torments). Jamaicans fondly remember a candy called Bustamante Jawbone in reference to the imagined toughness of the jawbone of that country's famous statesman known for his oratory. Then there's the poetic callaloo, matoutou, blaff, crasé, souse, lambi, and malanga.

While roadside stands are wonderful and small restaurants will give you an authentic taste of Caribbean food, the best place of all to eat in the islands is Sunday dinner at someone's grandmother's home. Here food takes on an almost ritual importance. Each meal is created lovingly . . . slow-cooked and well seasoned. No matter how humble, the meal itself is a feast. And from the first drop of rum—traditionally poured for the ancestors who are also present—through the crunch of the last bone being savored, to the final after-dinner drink; the heated conversation; and the almost obligatory after-dinner nap, it becomes clear what Caribbean dining is all about: food, friends, and fellowship.

A

CULINARY

HISTORY

OF THE

CARIBBEAN

ARAWAKS AND CARIBS:
FOOD BEFORE COLUMBUS

The culinary history of the Caribbean region began long before Columbus's arrival in this hemisphere. The two major groups of Native Americans occupying the islands, the Arawaks and the Caribs, had no trouble surviving on the bounty of the land. The Arawaks, gentle and peaceful as the history texts tell it, were cultivators who grew sweet potatoes, yautia, maize, peanuts, and cassava. The cassava bread that is eaten in the entire region owes its origin to these people. They are known to have enjoyed naseberries, guavas, pineapples, cashew fruit, and more.

The Arawaks were also hunters, and they enjoyed agouti (called grass cutter or bush rat in Africa), iguana, and jutia (a type of large guinea pig). They cooked fish that they caught in local rivers and streams. They were particularly adept at trapping ducks and other waterfowl. They would float gourds downriver until the fowl became adjusted to their presence in the water. The Arawak would then swim in the ponds or lakes using calabash gourds as rebreathers and sneak up on the unwitting fowl, yanking them under by the feet. The Arawak showed equal cleverness hunting for turtle. They would catch a remora or sucker fish, attach it to a long line, and then go turtle fishing. The fish would dive for the turtle and attach itself. They would reel in the fish and voilà . . . turtle stew!

The Arawak baked, stewed, smoked, and roasted their meats, frequently seasoning them with cassareep, a condiment prepared from cassava juice, salt, and pepper. It is used today in preparing pepperpot in Guyana, Trinidad, and Grenada. The grill of green wood sticks that they used to cook meats over an open fire was called a *barbacoa*. This style of cooking, the barbecue, lives on in the humble backyard grills and sophisticated mesquite and grapevine fires that have become so much a part of warm-weather culinary life in the States. The Arawak may also have been the first in the region to ferment alcohol, preparing potent beverages of cassava and maize.

The fierce Caribs, who occupied the northwest part of Trinidad, the Lesser Antilles, and the eastern part of Puerto Rico, were devoted meat eaters. They were also cannibals, and so all too frequently the cookpots were not only filled with the wild boars that ran in the virgin forests of the area, but also with the Arawak neighbors, captured in local skirmishes. The Caribs ate much the same as their neighbors, but with the accent on protein. They eschewed turtle meat and pork, feeling that the former would render them stupid and the latter caused people to have beady eyes. Crabmeat was never eaten before a long ocean voyage as it was thought to bring tempests.

However, in matters culinary, the Caribs are perhaps best known as lovers of things spicy; they seasoned their food with pepper only and did not use salt. It is perhaps from the Caribs that the region gains its fondness for pepper sauces. Sauces such as *taumalin,* which was made from pepper, lemon juice, and crabmeat, were typical. The Caribs also didn't mind a little drink from time to time. An intoxicating beverage called *ouicou* was prepared from cassava, sweet potatoes, and syrup and imbibed on holidays.

•

EXPLORERS, MISSIONARIES, AND BUCCANEERS

Columbus's arrival in the New World signaled a change in the diets of both the Old and New worlds. New World vegetables such as tomatoes, corn, chiles, and more would make their way eastward to become integral parts of European, African, and Asian cooking. Those continents in turn would supply the islands with other foodstuffs. Rice came from the East; bananas arrived from the Canary Islands in 1516, thanks to the Portuguese. The sugarcane that would make the region's fortune in the seventeenth, eighteenth, and early nineteenth centuries arrived with Columbus on his second voyage. Many other fruits and vegetables found their way to the area in the sixteenth, seventeenth, and eighteenth centuries, including breadfruit, which was brought by Captain Bligh of *Bounty* fame in 1793. Much of the culinary cross-pollinating was done by Jesuit missionaries, who never can receive enough praise in cookbooks for their hand in making many staples such as chiles international.

The subsequent wars for supremacy in the region would be aided by privateers and buccaneers, each of whom added something to the culinary lexicon. The former fought with the commission of their government and were considered to be heroes in their homelands. The latter gained their name from their preference for meat smoked in the native manner called *boucan.* They were first known as *boucaniers* and then buccaneers.

Pirates flying the skull and crossbones of the *Jolly Roger* owed allegiance to no government and harried any ship they found. They too haunted the coves and hidden harbors of the region, looking for treasures from the Spanish Main journeying to Europe. The region's pirates rapidly gained a fondness for the local tipple, a drink known as *Guildivel* or Kill Devil. It was strong and cheap; a half century later it would be refined into rum and become the drink most emblematic of the region.

Jean-Baptiste Labat, a Dominican monk, was an early French missionary to the region. His tales of his voyage to the American islands and his stay from 1694 to 1705 are riveting reading for anyone interested in the early culinary history of the area. Père Labat developed a taste for native barbecue and was also extremely fond of local turtles. His writings give us some of the most precise details that we have about the cooking of the Arawaks and the Caribs. He was an indefatigable observer and apparently quite the gourmet (not to mention gourmand). He came, he saw, he sampled. He also wrote detailed descriptions in his diaries of the foods of the late seventeenth and early eighteenth centuries.

Labat speaks of a meal of roasted turtle breast that he had eaten with all of the gustatory sensitivity of a Brillat-Savarin. He describes the preparation of the dish in such detail that the recipe could be easily duplicated today. The turtle breast was prepared with a marinade of lemon juice, chile, pepper, salt, and cloves and then basted with the marinade while roasting. He then goes on to allow that turtle meat is very versatile and can be prepared in a variety of ways: spit-roasted, stewed, fricasseed, in soup, and more. The missionary also gives the reader a detailed account of the fruits and vegetables in his garden and describes okra, cassava, Congo peas, sorrel, pineapples, bananas, and avocados, all of which were exotic vegetables to most Europeans well into the twentieth century. It is astonishing how similar many of the scenes described and the dishes sampled are to those of today's Caribbean.

●

SIR LOIN, KING SUGAR, AND DEMON RUM: THE PLANTATION KITCHEN

Culinary excess was one of the hallmarks of the plantation era in the Caribbean. Eyewitness accounts of lavish parties, expansive breakfasts, and groaning-board feasts are leitmotifs of the travelers' tales of the period. The expression "as rich as a Barbados planter" was common during this period and only hinted at all of the luxurious excess that the sugar-monied *nouveau riche* could buy. Lady Nugent, the wife of the governor of Jamaica, made a tour of the island from 1801 to 1805 and was astounded by the diet. She reported in her diary that all meals on the plantation were copious and made up of rich foods—roasts, smoked fish, meats, and more were present on the slave-carved mahogany tables and sideboards. These meals also offered a variety of spirits as well, all of which when combined with the torpor-inspiring climate of the region resulted in the plantation owners often eating themselves—quite literally —to death.

Eyewitness reports have it that many a master's day began with a mixture of Madeira wine and water upon rising. According to John Stedman, who reported on life in the British West Indies in 1772 in *A Planter's Day*: "a master's breakfast was at 10 o'clock for which his table is spread in the large hall provided, with bacon, ham, hung beef, fowls, or pigeons broiled; plantains and sweet cassavas roasted, bread, butter, cheese, etc. with which he drinks strong beer, and a glass of Madeira, Rhenish, or Mozell [sic] wine . . . and this is called breaking the poor man's fast." By 3 o'clock in the afternoon, it is time for dinner "where nothing is wanting that the world can afford in a western climate of meat, fowl, venison, fish, vegetables, fruits, etc. and the most exquisite wines are often squandered in profusion . . . after this, a cup of strong coffee and a liqueur finish the repast." The evening would finish up with "weak punch, sangaree, cards and tobacco."

Another report chronicles that "custards, cheesecakes, tansies, sturgeon, anchovies, caviar, boltards, tongues, peas, beans, several roasts and other good dishes" were all a part of the planter's lifestyle. Indeed, rich colonists reveled in their excellent tables, and shops vied for their patronage, purveying the most exotic of imported goods. A shop in Spanish Town, Jamaica, lured customers in 1781 by advertising "claret, hock, Yorkshire hams and the best mustard along with ladies and men's wear and clothing and household furnishings."

In the British colonies, taverns and coffeehouses catered to the male of the species in Hogarthian splendor, while Creole women in the French islands and plantation mistresses everywhere preferred to stay at home and enjoy chocolate, candies, coffee with milk, and a lemonade prepared from sugar syrup and lemon juice.

Entertaining was the perfect excuse to pull out all the stops. The choicest meats were prepared in the style of the prevailing colonial power and accompanied by a variety of sauces both in the European and creole manners. These were joined on the menu by vegetables both local and imported and accompanied by breads prepared from wheat flour and the local cassava flour that had become quite popular. The meal was washed down by veritable tidal waves of the finest wines and liquors available. Next came a selection of cheeses and savories imported from Europe, followed by desserts, ranging from British trifles to candied tropical fruits.

The settings were as lavish as the dishes served. Liveried slaves carrying torches lined entranceways bordered by majestic royal palm trees. At the great houses, which were invariably set high on hills in order to catch the few cool breezes and to have a better vantage point from which to watch for hints of unusual slave activities, wide verandas alight with silver candelabra offered panoramic vistas of acres of sugarcane fields. Household servants circulated soundlessly on polished mahogany floors, carrying heavy silver trays of predinner tidbits, proffering the punches that were symbolic of Caribbean hospitality, and seeing to the comfort of the invited guests. At the more lavish gatherings, miniature lakes of punches complete with slaves in rowboats serving the guests were not unheard of as party highlights. European visitors marveled at the sumptuous entertaining styles of Caribbean planters, and however appalled they might have been by the diet or by the slave condition that allowed for such ostentation, they uniformly agreed that "hospitality is in no country practiced with greater cordiality."

•

COAL POTS AND CALABASHES: THE SLAVE KITCHEN

In a parallel and enslaved society, African slaves brought with them the tastes and foods of their homeland. More fortunate than many of their brethren who were shipped to the United States, Caribbean slaves discovered a climate that mirrored that of their African home on the other side of the Atlantic. The familiar climate enabled them to easily transplant and acclimatize many African fruits and vegetables or discover New World equivalents. Okra, yams, sweet potatoes, greens, and at least ten types of beans all appeared in the earthenware and cast-iron pots that they used for cooking.

The nourishment of slaves, while not always considered a priority by unscrupulous planters, was a matter of great concern for colonial administrators of the period. Article 22 of France's Code Noire of 1685, which governed matters concerning slave welfare in the French colonies, provided that "slaves ten years and above be given two and a half measures of manioc flour or three cassavas weighing two and a half pounds each (or the equivalent) with two pounds of salt beef or three pounds of fish or other viands in like proportion and for children under ten years, half the above ration." Article 23 goes on to forbid planters giving rum instead of the rations mentioned. This was done because the rum was cheaper and the beverage's euphoria enabled the slaves to work with empty bellies. Article 24 of the Code Noire goes on to ensure that slaves had the right to complain if they were not so nourished and state that plantation owners found guilty of such abuses could be prosecuted.

In the British colonies, the system of slave kitchen gardens was instituted and maintained from an early date. Indeed, Sunday markets where the produce from these gardens was sold or traded for other items were so popular that they lasted well past emancipation and became a veritable fixture of rural life on some islands.

Back in the slave quarters of numerous Caribbean big houses, slaves reverted to African ways of cooking as well. Charcoal fires burning in tripod coal pots scented many a slave kitchen or market with the aroma of foods cooking over wood. Banana leaves served for wrapping foods to be steamed. Heavy cast-iron cooking pots called dutchies in Jamaica, buckpots or black pots in Barbados, and various other names in other islands were the cooking vessels of choice. Earthenware jugs called monkey pots kept water cool, while calabash gourds were used everywhere for everything from dishes to dippers.

With these tools, slave cooks produced dishes such as coocoo and funghi, relatives of the West African fufus and foutous; callaloo, a close cousin of the sauces feuilles of Benin and the *gumbo z'herbes* of New Orleans, and matoutou crabes, a traditional Easter dish in the French Antilles that is a direct descendant of Benin's ago glain. They went into the woods and found herbs and grasses from which they produced bush teas and used the sugarcane that marked their lives to make candies and hard sweet cakes. At times, they reproduced their African dishes in name and preparation as with West Africa's Akan people, who reproduced Ghana's kenkey and dokono as Barbados's conkies and Jamaica's dunkanoo. Other times they added a New World creole touch as with Martinique tabara, which has its origins in Senegal. In short, they gave the area new foods and methods of cooking, ones emblematic of another type of Caribbean cooking that has the indelible mark of Africa on it.

•

ROTI AND PAK CHOI:
FOODS FROM THE EAST

The postemancipation period brought a wave of immigration to the Caribbean area from India and China. The new Caribbean immigrants would bring with them their own vegetables, such as the Chinese bok choy, which is spelled pak choi in the Caribbean. They put down roots in Jamaica, Trinidad, Martinique, Grenada, Santo Domingo, and Cuba. They would use their own culinary techniques and the new ingredients that they found to create combinations such as Martinique's *colombo de porc*. A curried pork dish that would receive frowns from devout Hindus in India, it displays Caribbean ingenuity in combining the traditional southern Indian curry with pork, one of the most abundant meats in the region. Another example is Guyana's chop suey, which, like its American counterpart, owes little, except its name, to China. Visitors to Trinidad are surprised to find reminders of this culinary thread on virtually every street corner as vendors hawk what has become Trinidad's favorite snack food: *roti*. The dish consists of a crepelike pancake wrapper around a variety of curried fillings: chicken, lamb, beef, or vegetable.

While most travelers are not journeying to Cuba, those living in areas with a sizable Cuban population cannot help but be aware of yet another trend from the East, the *comidas chinas y criollas*. This type of cooking offers a wide array of foods that demonstrate the coming together of Spanish and Chinese culinary traditions with the produce of the tropics.

Few people today realize, as they munch on a bag of spicy *channa,* roasted chick-peas, purchased from a street vendor in Georgetown, Guyana, or pick up a roasted chicken dusted with egg powder and seasoned with hoisin sauce at a market in Kingston, Jamaica, or add a dab of kuchela, a shaved mango condiment, to their roti in San Fernando, Trinidad, that they are sampling the offerings of yet another continent in the melting pot that is Caribbean cooking.

•

CONTINENTAL DRIFT: TOURISM'S TOURMENTS

In the 1940s and '50s tourism was a fledgling industry in the Caribbean. By the 1960s and early '70s no influence was greater on the Caribbean kitchen than that of tourism. The tastes of the hordes (or in many cases anticipated hordes) of visitors from the North would put hamburgers, pizza, Coca-Cola, fried chicken, and the like on the tables of many hotel dining rooms. "Continental" cuisine was the watchword. The modified American plan (MAP) meant that guests ate at the hotel at least twice a day and guests should not be bothered with the unfamiliar. Local food was anathema, to be avoided at all costs. It was only to be encountered if you were lucky enough to be invited to someone's home.

These are the Dark Ages of Caribbean culinary history. However, no

Dark Age is so complete that it does not have its glimmer of light. This era produced some of the region's best-known cocktails. The piña colada, today's classic tropical vacation drink, is a product of this era. The daiquiri and the Andrews Sisters' famed Rum and Coca-Cola also hark back to the early part of this period. Some of the more famous hangouts of the era were Cuba's La Bodeguita del Medio, where autographed walls are a testimony to pre-Castro glory days. The Mojito, a rum, spearmint, and tonic water drink said to be a favorite of Ernest Hemingway is this bistro's legacy. In another part of Havana, La Floridita beckons as the home of the daiquiri, although the drink's origins are also attributed to workers on the sugar plantation at the Daiquiri iron mines. The pioneer Caribe Hilton of Puerto Rico, which can claim to be the first hotel of the Caribbean tourism boom, has added many rum cocktails to the list, although its claim to the piña colada is disputed among several locations.

The end of the period marked a Caribbean awareness that tourism was probably going to be the wave of the future. Culinary competitions were organized by newly independent governments and encouraged chefs in restaurants and hotel dining rooms to experiment with local produce in a thrust toward self-sufficiency. Meanwhile, in the north, Julia Child was changing the country's approach to food. As inquiring taste buds raced their way through French, Italian, Chinese, Indian, and regional American foods including Cajun and California, and headed onward to Thai, Vietnamese, Mexican, and Moroccan foods, it became clear that the tidal wave of the culinary revolution would soon wash ashore on the Caribbean islands.

•

CARIBBEAN RENAISSANCE: TODAY'S CREOLE FEASTS

The late 1980s heralded a new feeling of pride in the Caribbean, resulting in a rediscovery of traditional Caribbean cuisine. In the United States, Caribbean restaurants have emerged from urban ethnic neighborhoods to present the population-at-large with a glimpse of the diversity of this cuisine. Meanwhile, in the islands, growing health consciousness, higher standards of living, and more discerning tourists are transforming the cuisine. Traditional dishes are being reevaluated, refined, and reinstated on resort and restaurant menus. Chefs are looking to local produce and the diverse seafood of the region for inspiration. Ackee and saltfish can be found on numerous Jamaican breakfast buffets, while in Guadeloupe féroce d'avocat, a spicy avocado and codfish dip, with *mignan de fruit à pain* (pureed breadfruit) might be offered. Dinner in the Dominican Republic might bring a bread basket with warm *pan de casabe* (cassava bread) while tea in Barbados might present coconut tartlets along with more traditional fare.

Restaurants highlight the region's traditional food. Mama's in Grenada serves a smorgasbord of traditional foods, including such delicacies as iguana, armadillo, and monkey. De Armando in Puerto Plata, Dominican Republic, offers *crema de auyama* (pumpkin soup) and *moro choncho* (rice and beans with pork) on its extensive menu. Martinique and Guadeloupe are veritable gourmets' paradises for lovers of traditional creole cooking. The latter island's annual Fête des Cuisinières gives tasters one of the best samplings of the food of the French Caribbean around. And don't forget the Dutch. When they say, *"Bon probecho!"*, Papamiento for *"Bon appétit,"* they sit down to dishes like *erwten soep,* a pea soup that speaks of their heritage, and may follow it up with *passaat,* a lamb or goat barbecue where the flames are fanned by the island tradewinds, or *passaat.*

As it heads toward the twenty-first century, the cooking of the Caribbean whether nouvelle or traditional, langouste or lambi, offers diners from around the world a melting pot of delights, a veritable creole feast.

CREOLE FEAST: AN ISLAND- BY- ISLAND LOOK AT CARIBBEAN COOKING

Since visitors to the Caribbean region tend to take in one or two islands at a time or else travel on cruise ships where they do not have a chance to sample much local cooking, most do not realize that Caribbean cooking varies from island to island. Each island has its specialties and its own culinary quirks.

•

ANGUILLA

Miles of beaches and restaurants selling all of the sea's bounty make Anguilla a seafood lover's dream. The island's specialties—lobster of the clawless Caribbean type, crayfish, whelk, yellowtail, and red snapper—are all freshly caught from local cays and reefs and brought to the table still perfumed with the taste of the sea. Shellfish turns up in traditional grilled and other classic guises at many island restaurants and in more innovative forms at places like Pimm's on Maunday's Bay and Hibernia, where crab beignets, lobster tabbouleh, and conch torte can be found.

•

ANTIGUA AND BARBUDA

Along with its importance in British naval history, Antigua has always been at the forefront with things culinary. In fact, the Antiguan black pineapple figures on the country's coat of arms. This pineapple, which is being revived after virtually disappearing, is small, dark skinned, and very sweet because of its high sucrose content. The pineapples can be purchased in local markets for on-island enjoyment, and locally made pineapple products such as jams and preserves can be purchased in local supermarkets. The classic Antiguan dish, though, is pepperpot, one of the traditional Caribbean soups. The Antiguan pepperpot, however, has more vegetables than its namesakes on other islands and uses chicken, beef, or pork rather than crabmeat. Antiguans are also fond of their funghi, a boiled cornmeal mush cake traditionally served with boiled fish. Dishes are frequently seasoned with one of the incendiary hot sauces for which the island and indeed the region is also known. For most visitors, Antigua's nautical history is vividly conjured up by Nelson's Dockyard. The connection between British naval history and rum is a lifeline that runs throughout the culinary history of Antigua and the Caribbean. Local rums can be found and tours of the distilleries can be arranged in advance.

•

ARUBA

Visitors to Aruba are usually more concerned with the odds at the gaming tables and the amount of daily sunshine than they are with the island's numerous restaurants. However, when eat they must, breaded conch; *pan bati,* a cornmeal and flour pancake; fried plantains; and red snapper Aruban-style are some of the local specialties available. In addition, one of the island's drawing points for those who love food are the diverse locales of the island's numerous restaurants, ranging from landmark lighthouses to historic plantation houses to Dutch windmills to a houseboat. The cuisines to be sampled run the gamut from the traditional creole cooking of Aruba, which mixes African and Dutch cooking in dishes such as *sopito,* a fish soup flavored with coconut, to Indonesian rijstaffel, which hails from the other end of the former Dutch empire.

•

THE BAHAMAS

Conch, pronounced "conk," is the pivot post of Bahamian cuisine. People recommend it as a cure for everything from hangnails to sexual deficiencies. Conch, a large mollusk, is found in restaurants all over the country, but true aficionados head for Potter's Cay under the bridge to Paradise Island, where conch lovers and photographers alike enjoy watching the local conchmongers open a fresh conch. The conch meat is mixed with a squeeze of lime, raw onion, and fiery Bahamian bird peppers. Usually the mixture is eaten out of a plastic bag as a late breakfast or a "restorative" after a late night. Boiled fish and stewed fish, two local ways of preparing fish, are also breakfast favorites and are frequently eaten with johnny cakes or grits. *Souse,* a lime juice, pepper, and onion marinade that can season anything from pig's knuckles and tails to chicken wings, is a popular treat, as are all manner of tropical fruits.

The ubiquitous conch returns later in the day as conch fritters or "crack conch," a Bahamian variation on the Caribbean fritter theme that finds itself as *acras* in Martinique and Guadeloupe and as *bacalaitos* in Puerto Rico. They are served as appetizers or as *amuse-gueules* during drinks and are often accompanied by tartar sauce or local red hot sauce made from bird peppers.

Food lovers who wish to get another feeling for Bahamian food outside of the island's restaurants should take a chance with the lunches sold by women out of their car trunks at lunch hour in Nassau. The portions of chicken, mutton, ribs, and fried fish with peas and rice or potato salad as side dishes tell more about Bahamian food than any cookbook or restaurant could.

●

BARBADOS

Unlike many of the other Caribbean countries, Barbados has been under one European influence since its initial colonization—British. It is here that the empire of Sir Loin and the realm of King Sugar come together. The result is a style of cooking that mixes the heartiness of British fare with the spiciness of things African, one that combines the bounty of local fruits and vegetables with the wealth of local waters. Two dishes are emblematic of the cooking of Barbados: pudding and souse, the traditional Saturday supper dish, and flying fish. Pudding is well-seasoned sweet potato that is placed in a sausage casing and steamed; and the souse is a spicy mixture of pig's feet, snouts, and tails (and more) served in a lime juice marinade along with green bell peppers, cucumber, onion slices, parsley, and fiery hot Capsicum chiles. Flying fish is usually served lightly breaded and pan-fried accompanied by a tartar sauce.

The quintessential Barbadian buffet is the one served at Sunday brunch at the Atlantis Hotel in Bathsheba. The hotel is one of the oldest on the island and the brunch is a local favorite offering everything from spinach fritters and fried breadfruit to coconut pie. As elsewhere in the Caribbean, rum is the typical drink and Barbados produces several brands, notably Mount Gay and Cockspur. On Wednesdays, it is possible to visit the Mount Gay factory and watch the rum being produced.

BONAIRE

The lure of the sea is what brings most people to Bonaire. The island's diving is legendary. When the urge to eat does occur, the accent is once again on the fish; virtually everything else is imported. Lobster is a specialty and is served grilled at many island restaurants. Those wishing to explore a bit more of the island can take a trip to the salt ponds, which give an idea of one of the ways salt is produced and how this product affects Bonaire's economy.

BRITISH VIRGIN ISLANDS

The biggest lure of the British Virgin Islands is that they are relatively undiscovered. British influence is found in the cooking, but it is still possible to find numerous traditional West Indian items such as maubey, a nonalcoholic drink made from tree bark. This is served along with West Indian specialties at the Aires Club in Road Town on Tortola. Out on the island, the Sugar Mill restaurant, which is housed in a three-hundred-year-old sugar-processing plant, offers dinners that combine classic culinary techniques with tropical ingredients, such as mangoes, papayas, and fiery hot peppers. Also on Tortola, the Sunny Caribee Herb and Spice Company offers a wide selection of local spices and cure-alls ranging from crystallized ginger to a Caribbean hangover cure, all packaged in locally designed containers. The spirited side of the island culinary life is revealed in locally produced Pusser's rum.

CAYMAN ISLANDS

The Cayman Islands' original name of *Las Tortugas,* the turtles, speaks to the numerous wild turtles that Columbus found on the islands when he landed. Today, the turtles are rare in the wilds, but aquaculture, the farming of turtles, crayfish, and tropical freshwater fish, forms an integral part of the Cayman Islands' economy. Today's visitors to the Cayman Islands are tempted with all manner of international cuisines. Those wishing to have a taste of these islands' past can sample turtle steaks and turtle soup and visit the turtle farm on Grand Cayman.

●

CUBA

Few, if any, American tourists are currently traveling to this, the largest of all the Caribbean islands. Therefore, much of what we know today about Cuban food comes from the Cuban population that has migrated to the United States in the years following the Castro revolution. From them, we have learned of the delights of Cuban sandwiches; *lechón asado* (roast pig); *moros y cristianos,* Cuba's variation on rice and beans; and black bean soup. Most of us, though, have never tasted *ajiaco,* the Cuban national dish, which is what happened when the Spanish Olla Podrida met up with the Arawak pepper pot. We haven't sampled Cuba's African-inspired dishes, such as *quimbombo con pollo y bolas de platano* (a chicken and okra stew with plantain dumplings) or *chilindron de chivo* (a spicy goat stew), or *congri oriental* (a rice and kidney bean mixture seasoned with slab bacon, chorizo, cherry tomatoes, thyme, and bay leaf). We drink daiquiris and barely remember that they come from Daiquiri in Cuba and almost consider cubalibres passé, but we are only discovering the *mojito* (a rum, tonic water, sugar, and spearmint drink). Unfortunately, unless we live near a Cuban neighborhood in Florida, New York, or New Jersey, we're unlikely to taste Cuban ice cream, one of the world's frozen delights, or Cuban pastries from Santiago, a legacy of that city's settlers who fled from the Haitian revolution of 1804.

●

CURAÇAO

Curaçao, which in the minds of food lovers means not only the island but the liqueur, offers visitors a wide variety of cuisines including Dutch, Caribbean, Indonesian, Latin American, Chinese, and European. Traditional local dishes include *funchi,* corn pancakes that are eaten plain or with a variety of fillings, and *keshi yena,* an Edam cheese stuffed with meat, shrimp, or chicken and then baked. More esoteric dishes include *zult,* pickled pigs' ears, and *soppi juana,* iguana soup. All are washed down with Curaçao's own Amstel beer, which is brewed from desalinated sea water. The brew is so popular that the island population's consumption of it matches that of Holland and is four times that of neighboring Caribbean islands. Visitors to the island can tour the brewery.

However, in many minds, Curaçao means one thing—curaçao liqueur. The Spaniards are credited with the planting of the orange trees that would lead to the creation of this liqueur. The arid climate, however, produced a fruit that was inedible. It was only two hundred years later that the aromatic oil from the oranges was discovered to be perfect for flavoring foods and drinks and became the main ingredient in the locally produced liqueur that would become known as curaçao. Produced at Chobolo, one of Curaçao's surviving Dutch colonial *landhuis* farmhouses, the liqueur still uses the fruit of the descendants of the Spanish orange trees. Those touring the factory will learn that the only "original and authentic curaçao" comes in five different colors—clear, orange, amber, green, and blue—and that they all taste the same.

No food lover could visit Curaçao without a stop at the country's "floating" market where Venezuelan schooners bring fresh produce for the country's tables. A little farther up the street, it is possible to sample local foods cooked over charcoal fires near the old market.

•

DOMINICA

Dominica is said to be the only Caribbean island that Columbus would recognize if he were to return to the archipelago today. And indeed, while he might be familiar with the lush greenery, the food of the country bears witness to much history that has transpired since his arrival. Spanish, British, and French culinary traditions come together here. Perhaps the most noted local dish is crapaud or mountain chicken, as the immense island frogs are called. They are on the menu along with dishes such as crab back and ti-ti-ri (a whitebait-size local fish), at restaurants like madras-decorated La Robe Créole in Roseau.

THE DOMINICAN REPUBLIC

Beach, golf, and history are usually uppermost in the minds of most travelers to the Dominican Republic. However, most leave enchanted by the nation's variety of food. In Santo Domingo, the capital, restaurants abound with Spanish and Dominican cuisines in the spotlight. More surprisingly are the capital's excellent Chinese restaurants. Local Dominican dishes include hearty stews such as *sancocho,* a dish with an infinite number of varieties and ingredients; *lambi,* conch served in a multiplicity of ways; and the national dish, *chicharrón de pollo,* small pieces of marinated fried chicken. But for many, the ultimate Dominican taste is that of *chicharrón de cerdo con yuca,* a dish of crispy pork cracklings served with yuca. The moist sweet pork and the starchy yuca seasoned with a squirt of lemon juice are typical of what traditional Dominican dining is all about.

No visit to the Dominican Republic is complete without an introduction to the three B's—Barcelo, Brugal, and Bermudez, the Dominican Republic's three rums, which enliven virtually every Dominican meal. Those visiting in Puerto Plata can visit the bottling plant and watch as the rum is made.

•

GRENADA

Grenada, the Isle of Spice, is one of the world's largest producers of nutmeg and mace, and these spices run as a leitmotif through the cooking of the region. Banda nutmegs came to Grenada in 1843 via an English sea captain coming from Indonesia. Today, nearly half of the world's crop of nutmeg and mace, the outside aril encasing the nutmeg shell, comes from Grenada.

The island's cooking features a number of influences ranging from French through British with a hint of the Orient and even a dash from a growing number of American tourists. Hoteliers, particularly at properties like Blue Horizon and Calabash, have combined local produce and the abundance of local waters to create new dishes such as La Belle Créole's sweet potato soufflé.

For those who would love to sample the traditional cooking of the region, Grenada offers what is perhaps one of the Caribbean's most unusual tasting restaurants at Mama's. Mama's restaurant, located in Belmont near the capital of St. George's, offers a selection of nearly two dozen traditional Grenadian dishes on a prix fixe menu, ranging from the standard, fresh fish, to the unusual, *manicou* (opossum) and *tatoo* (armadillo) along with a selection of salads, curries, and exotic ice creams for dessert.

If Mama's offers one view of the Grenadian dining experience and restaurants such as Calabash and La Belle Créole offer another, a trip to Betty Mascoll's offers yet a third. At the gracious lady's plantation great house in Morne Fendue near Sauteurs, it is possible to arrange for a buffet luncheon which traditionally includes her famous pepper pot made dark and slightly sweet in the southern Caribbean style with cassareep, an inheritance from the Arawaks. Mascoll herself will regale guests with tales of great house life and anecdotes about Grenadian food.

•

GUADELOUPE

This is one of the culinary highpoints of the region for those who enjoy creole food in the French style (or simply French cooking in all of its permutations). Local specialties are *maçonne,* a kidney bean and rice dish flavored with spices, and even a variation on the turtle soup that so enchanted Père Labat in the late seventeenth and early eighteenth centuries. As the Creole proverb puts it: *Mie vaut vente peté ku mangé gaté* (It's better for your stomach to burst than to waste good food). Things culinary are given such a high place in the cultural activities of Guadeloupe that there is even an annual Feast of the Women Cooks, for the best creole cooks in Guadeloupe are traditionally women. The feast is celebrated on the second Saturday in August. Dressed in madras finery and laden with baskets adorned with the miniature tools of their trade, the cooks parade to the cathedral to attend a mass in their honor before adjourning to a nearby venue for feasting, dancing, and general good times. Their feast day, incidentally, coincides with that of Saint Lawrence. Why? His hagiography indicates that he was tortured by being grilled.

Easter Monday brings out families to local beaches where they set up their own cook pots and traditionally enjoy matété crabes, a dish descended from Benin's ago glain. The Christmas holidays bring in feasting in the French form with Antillean dishes added to the traditional réveillon dinners that are held on Christmas and New Year's eves. All year round visitors can stop at local markets to purchase spices, such as *bois d'inde* (allspice) and a local curry powder called *colombo,* from women with madras headties.

On Ile des Saintes, one of Guadeloupe's dependencies, the street snack of note is called *tourment d'amour,* love's torment. It is a coconut tart, which is sold by barefoot children near the pier where the ferry from Guadeloupe docks.

●

HAITI

Haitian cooking is distinctive from that of the other French-speaking areas of the Caribbean and mirrors the island's independent history. The country is divided into two distinct culinary regions with the northern area around Cap Haitien being known for its *cuisine du nord,* which features dishes cooked with cashew nuts. Traditional African-inspired dishes eaten by Haitians include *tum tum,* a pounded breadfruit or cornmeal mush similar to the *funghis* and *coocoos* of the English-speaking islands; these are dishes that visitors will find served in mainly private homes. Restaurant food features such Haitian dishes as *riz djon djon,* rice cooked with indigenous black mushrooms; *banane pesé,* deep-fried plantains; *grillots de porc,* deep-fried pork bits; *poisson gros sel,* red snapper seasoned with shallots, onions, and hot pepper; and *tassot dinde,* sun-dried turkey.

French culinary tradition is also honored here, and most places favor recipes from *cuisine bourgeoise:* tournedos bordelaise, langouste flambée, escargots bourguignonne. These dishes, sometimes featuring inventive uses of tropical produce, can be found at restaurants such as Chez Gérard and La Souvenance.

Those who wish to see what it takes to bring produce to market in Haiti have only to awaken early and watch the women coming down the roads from Kenscoff carrying baskets laden with everything from oranges and tangerines to strawberries, which can be grown in the more temperate Kenscoff area.

The Jane Barbancourt rum factory has long been a fixture on tours for many visitors to Haiti. The establishment, which can be described as a Baskin-Robbins for imbibers, offers for sale and sampling twenty varieties of rum-based liquors. In an afternoon, on the sun-filled balconies of the ersatz castle, it is possible to sample rum liqueurs flavored with everything from apricot and coconut to guava and hibiscus. Haiti's rum drinks may not be well known; however, Haiti's Rhum Barbancourt is world renowned.

JAMAICA

"Ackee, rice, saltfish are nice / and the rum is fine any time of year . . ." So says the calypso, and nothing could be truer of Jamaica. Here, indeed, is a country where the culinary traditions of the English, the Africans, and newer immigrants like the Lebanese and the Chinese have blended to produce a distinctive cuisine. Ackee, a local fruit, when combined with salted codfish, one of the region's seafaring legacies, produces the classic Jamaican breakfast. Rice might refer to the peas and rice that are found on so many tables they are laughingly referred to as the Jamaican coat of arms, and the rum . . . well, the rum is the hallmark of the island.

Traditional Jamaican food is increasingly in the forefront, as visitors to the country are sampling and enjoying it at local hotels. Dishes such as jerked pork and janga or peppered shrimp are prime luncheon treats, and numerous roadside pork pits provide vacationers with the choice of eating in or taking out. Travelers who are more adventurous can search out such traditional Jamaican dishes as curried goat and manish water or others with more evocative names, such as stamp and go, batter-fried saltfish fritters, and matrimony, a dessert blending orange slices and star apple fruit in cream. Many visitors arrive in Jamaica already familiar with some of the country's exported culinary products such as Blue Mountain coffee, which they can watch being harvested in the Blue Mountains. The country also offers numerous plantation tours. Several rums are produced in Jamaica and the distilleries can be visited, as can factories where local liqueurs such as Tía Maria and Sangsters are made.

•

MARTINIQUE

Martinique, along with her twin to the north, Guadeloupe, offers some of the best French creole cooking in the region. Menus fairly bristle with choices, including such creole classics as *crabes farcies,* bread-crumb–stuffed land crabs that are highly seasoned and baked in their shells; *blaff,* a fish poached in wine spiced with lime, garlic, onion, cloves, bay rum berries, thyme, and peppers; *boudin créole,* a local blood sausage; and *acras,* fluffy codfish fritters. Individual chefs have added their own touches, such as lobster vinaigrette and *soufflé de papaye* (papaya soufflé), and more to the culinary lexicon.

The cooking of Martinique and Guadeloupe differs slightly, but both spring from the mix of African and French culinary styles. While the cuisine of Guadeloupe takes its inspiration from Africa, that of Martinique is inspired more by the French. Restaurants such as Le Lafayette offer dishes such as grilled saddle of lamb served with a pâté of seasoned avocado, eggplant, and fried plantain, or flying fish with a pistou sauce.

No meal in Martinique should begin without a ti-punch, a rum drink comprised of rum, sugar syrup, and a squeeze of lime. Martinique produces excellent rum and distillery visits are possible. It is even possible to visit the Musée du Rhum Saint James in Sainte-Marie for some history and a tasting.

Those traveling out on the island and wishing to sample some of the best of local food should arrange for lunch at the Manoir de Beauregard in the south, an antique-laden inn outside of Sainte-Anne, or at one of the small restaurants in the north, such as Chez Mally near Basse-Pointe or Le Colibri near Morne des Esses.

●

MONTSERRAT

Montserrat is known as the Emerald Isle of the Caribbean, an appellation that goes back to the 1632 landing of Irish settlers from then English Saint Kitts. This heritage is kept up in a variety of ways, cultural, philatelic, and culinary. The phone book might have been lifted from one of the smaller Irish counties, shamrocks abound on stamps and on the country's seal, and this must be one of the few countries in the Caribbean to grow and eat white potatoes. Local dishes include mountain chicken, frog's legs, goat water stew, and curried mutton.

●

PUERTO RICO

One of the standard-bearers of Spanish-influenced cooking in the Caribbean, Puerto Rico boasts a rich culinary tradition that is gaining international renown. The culinary tradition of the island mixes the cuisine of the Spanish settlers with local ingredients and a dash of the inventiveness of the African slaves. Dishes such as *asopao,* a chicken and rice mixture that is quite similar to the paella of Spain's Valencia, and *lechón asado,* a roast suckling pig such as could be had in many of Avila's restaurants, are complemented by *sopa de quimbombo,* an okra soup, and *bacalaitos,* codfish fritters, which bring African tastes to the menu. Island chefs sauté achiote seeds, so prized by the native Taino indians, in oil to produce an orange-hued oil that is used similar to West African palm oil. Foods are frequently seasoned either with *adobo,* a marinade of lemon or vinegar, garlic, pepper, salt, and spices, or a mixture known as *sofrito,* which is made of sautéed onions, garlic, and green pepper.

Restaurants in Old San Juan such as La Zaragozana, La Fonda del Callejon, and La Malloriquina offer a taste of some of Puerto Rico's and Spain's traditional dishes. Others in San Juan's hotels and around the island offer nouvelle Puerto Rican cuisine. Those traveling around the country can sample Puerto Rico's regional specialties at the island's numerous *paradors* (government-run inns) or visit the local saint's day festivities, such as the Fiestas Padronales de Santiago Apostal, which is held in Loiza Aldea each July. There it is possible to sample *empanadas de jueyes* (crab cakes) coconut water, and bacalaitos while listening to *bombas,* African couplets sung to the accompaniment of drum music.

No Caribbean island of any size would be complete without a rum distillery, and Puerto Rico produces many varieties of the area's emblematic beverage. It is possible to visit the distilleries and sample as well as purchase the wide variety of local rums.

•

SABA

The island known by aficionados as the big green gumdrop is the place to go for rest and relaxation. Quaint inns, with peace as their only offering, beckon. Island culinary specialties include hearty dinners served at Queenie Simmons Serving Spoon where the menu changes daily and the offerings are qualified simply as "a plate of food" and a local liqueur— Saba Spice, a potent mixture of nutmeg, rum, and "secret ingredients."

SAINT BARTHÉLEMY

French creole cuisine is in the forefront of cooking on Guadeloupe and Martinique, but on St. Barts, the accent is on La Belle France. The small island boasts over sixty restaurants serving dishes ranging from grilled lobster and steak to haute cuisine prepared by chefs trained in some of France's best kitchens. St. Barts can even boast two cooking schools: the Saint Barts Cooking School, which specializes in classical French cuisine, and Cooking in Paradise, which offers instruction in creole cuisine, fish dishes, and tropical desserts.

SAINT CROIX

The largest of the U.S. Virgin Islands, St. Croix is neither as urban as Saint Thomas nor as unspoiled as Saint John. Those looking for genuine Cruzan cooking can find it in small restaurants around Christiansted. This cuisine is frequently distinguished by the use of Cruzan seasoning, a mixture of fresh thyme, pepper, chives, and salt, which is rubbed onto meats and poultry before they are grilled. Traditional food with a great house flair can be had at Spratt Hall, the oldest continuously inhabited great house on the island. Here in the dining room, which was once the mansion's ballroom, visitors can dine on classical West Indian cooking served on the family china.

Cruzan rum is rapidly gaining popularity abroad.

SAINT JOHN

Two-thirds of Saint John is devoted to the Virgin Island National Park and given over to divers and nature enthusiasts. The remaining third boasts two elegant resorts: Caneel Bay and the Virgin Grand, and houses or condominiums for rent. The accent is on relaxation and enjoyment of nature, and culinary pickings are slim. Small restaurants and snack bars do give an opportunity to sample local fare, while the resorts offer dining in the European style.

•

SAINT KITTS AND NEVIS

Traditional dishes on St. Kitts and Nevis speak little of the country's history. They usually combine locally grown vegetables such as breadfruit, chayote (which is called christophine here), eggplant, and okra in stews and sauces that accompany local fish with names like blue parrot and kingfish. However, when these traditional dishes are transformed at the Golden Lemon, near Dieppe Bay on Saint Kitts, they evoke the turbulent history of the island. French, English, and African culinary influences are all in evidence.

In Basseterre, on Saint Kitts, Kittitian Kitchen sells homemade jams, jellies, and chutneys, and fruit and spice teas, along with handmade household items such as trays, coasters, napkin holders, baskets, and more. Out on the island, the past comes to life during crop time, when sugarcane is being harvested. Then it is possible to arrange tours to the Sugar Factory to watch the sugar trains come in laden with cane. On Nevis, the New River Estate was the last sugar mill to grind sugar. It can be visited, and its machinery is still in place. CSR, a local spirit, is a crystal-clear beverage distilled from fresh cane.

•

SAINT LUCIA

St. Lucia offers a mix of French, English, and creole cooking with specialties such as banana bread, fried plantain, boiled cucumbers, and pumpkin soup. Dishes are hearty and make frequent use of root vegetables such as African yam and dasheen. Traditional cooks on St. Lucia use coal pots for cooking. The heavy clay vessels are filled with hot coals and are typical of much African cooking in the Caribbean. From Saint Lucia's English-speaking past comes a callaloo thick with fresh spinach and flavored with salted beef. French creole influences bring *pouile Dudon*, a sweet, spicy chicken dish, and *tablette*, a coconut sugar candy.

Rain, one of Castries' leading restaurants, nightly re-creates an 1885 champagne banquet served to members of the Castries Philharmonic Society. San Antoine, in a restored great house overlooking Castries, features such dishes as escargots in choux pastry, smoked salmon mousse, and hazelnut meringue cake.

•

SINT MAARTEN/SAINT MARTIN

Dining seems to be a major preoccupation on the bi-national island of Sint Maarten/Saint Martin. Whether on the Dutch or the French side, restaurants abound, but the sole traces of Holland's empire can be found in Indonesian food, which is represented by the island's only rijstaffel at Wajong Doll on Front Street.

While a few years ago visitors to the French side, Saint Martin, would find only a few restaurants in Marigot and the famous "Ma" Chance's in Gran'Case, today both towns boast a veritable restaurant row, with offerings from French to creole to Italian to Vietnamese.

•

SAINT THOMAS

The most urban of the U.S. Virgin Islands offers visitors a wide selection of cuisines. At first look, it would seem impossible to find traditional West Indian cooking among the numerous restaurants. While inventive chefs at restaurants such as the Agave Terrace at the Point Pleasant Resort use local ingredients to enhance nouvelle cuisine meals, those diners wishing for a more authentic taste of St. Thomas should head for French Town outside of Charlotte Amalie, where restaurants like Johnnycakes and Eunice's serve callaloo, boiled fish and funghi, breadfruit, and lethal rum punches.

SAINT VINCENT AND
THE GRENADINES

A yachtsman's paradise is the way that St. Vincent and the Grenadines describe themselves. Indeed Saint Vincent, Young Island, Bequia, Mustique, and the rest offer a calm that is rapidly disappearing from the Caribbean scene. Local restaurants are always small and quirky, such as Mac's Pizzeria on Bequia, known for its lobster pizza, and Basil's Bar and Raft Restaurant on Mustique. Local food seems to have taken a bit from all of the culinary traditions that have crossed in the islands and encompasses everything from rum punch to pommes frites.

One culinary landmark to the history of sailing in the Caribbean is Captain Bligh's breadfruit tree. The story has it that the famous mutiny on the *Bounty* was caused because Bligh spent more time and gave more water to the breadfruit trees than he did to his crew. Following his unsuccessful voyage, he did return to the South Seas from whence he brought the breadfruit tree, a spur of which proudly stands in the Botanic Gardens in Kingstown on Saint Vincent.

TRINIDAD AND TOBAGO

Indian, Chinese, African, Spanish, French, and British influences all come together in Trinidad's melting pot. Callaloo—the soup that is traditional to the Caribbean—is so important here that it became the theme of a carnival band one year. Other traditional dishes that have not yet made carnival status but that are well loved just the same are *coocoo,* a steamed breadfruit or cornmeal pudding that is eaten covered with a sauce or accompanying steamed fish; *pelau,* an East meets West creolized pilaf; and *roti,* a crepelike Indian pancake wrapped around a curry mixture. Indian sweets and savories such as *channa,* pepper-flavored roasted chickpeas, are favorite snacks. *Tatoo,* a wild armadillo, and *manicou,* opossum, also find their way to the dining table stewed or fried and served in a sauce. The cascadura, a local fish reputed to make those who eat it return to Trinidad, has even become the subject of a work by Trinidadian writer Samuel Selvon.

On Tobago, dining is mainly in the hotels. The Blue Crab in Scarborough, the capital, however, offers traditional specialties.

●

TURKS AND CAICOS

Restaurants tend to be expensive because much of the food has to be imported. On Grand Turk there are places such as the Regal Beagle where British fare like fish and chips can be had. Those in search of local foods can go to Pillary beach where turtle stew is the specialty. Other island delicacies include conch fritters; conch stew; conch salad; turtle; spiny lobster; and fresh fish such as grouper, snapper, and wahoo. On Provo, local dishes are found at Le Deck, the Banana Boat, and Fast Eddie's.

INGREDIENTS

AND

UTENSILS:

A

GLOSSARY

Caribbean cooking calls for some ingredients that you may not be immediately familiar with, though most are readily available. For some, however, you'll have to take a trip to the Caribbean section of town where the greengrocers' stalls will be filled with greens such as those of the malanga and an abundance of tubers and root vegetables. There you'll also be able to find the incendiary chiles that are so emblematic of the region's cooking. In the meat markets, you'll find tripe and goat along with the more usual chicken and hams. Canned goods and staples available in the supermarkets will include twenty-five-pound bags of rice, canned ackee, and half-pound bags of special Madras curry powder.

Because Caribbean cooking takes in four languages, multiple cultures, and untold dialects, it's sometimes difficult to know what's what. One market's Scotch Bonnet chiles are another market's Haitian peppers and yet another market's habañeros. Assembled here is a wide variety of names and the Latin to help.

• ACHIOTE *BIXA ORELLANA* •

These small reddish berries are sometimes called annatto, urucu, or roucou and were used by the early Caribbean Indians to decorate their bodies. The berries still serve as a colorant today in the cooking of the Spanish-speaking Caribbean. There, they are mixed with lard or other cooking oils to give the oil and the foods cooked in them an orangish yellow coloring. It is difficult to document, but it has been suggested that this method of cooking first developed as a means of replacing the reddish-hued palm oil prized in much West African cooking. Achiote appears in the sofritos of the Spanish-speaking Caribbean and in the blaffs and the mignans of the French-speaking islands.

Achiote seeds should be purchased when they have a bright brick-reddish color. Once they have turned brown, they have lost much of their already faint flavor. The seeds may be kept indefinitely in a tightly covered jar in the refrigerator or in a cool, dark place.

• ACKEE *BLIGHIA SAPIDA* •

A Jamaican riddle asks: "My father sent me out to pick out a wife; he told me to take only those that smile, for those that do not smile will kill me. What is my wife?" The answer, as every Jamaican child knows, is ackee. The fruit looks a bit like a large pink mango or guava until it has ripened. Then it "smiles": bursting open, exposing yellow meat with its characteristic black seeds. Until the ackee has ripened naturally and is "smiling," it is poisonous. Ackee's yellow flesh has a scrambled-egg look. It is found most frequently in ackee and saltfish, the Jamaican national breakfast dish.

While Jamaicans have to worry about ackee "smiling," those of us in northern climes do not. As here, ackee is most frequently found in canned form.

• ALLSPICE *PIMENTA DIOICA, SYN. PIMENTA OFFICINALIS* •

This berry, the size of a large peppercorn, has the taste of nutmeg, cinnamon, black pepper, and cloves. The berries are also known as Jamaica pepper and, to the eternal confusion of many, as pimento. In the French-speaking Caribbean, allspice is known as *bois d'Inde* and is used extensively to season seafood dishes called blaffs and creole blood sausage. Other parts of the tree are also used. The leaves, which are similar to European bay leaves, appear in spice baskets in Grenada and on other islands. Even the wood is used: True Jamaican jerked foods are grilled over a fire of allspice branches, which gives the foods their characteristic flavor.

• AMCHAR •

This Indian addition to the cooking of Trinidad and Tobago is prepared from green mangoes or tamarind. It is traditionally served as an accompaniment to roti and many of the Trinidadian curries.

• ARROWROOT *MARANTA ARUNDINACEA* •

This rhizome is dried and powdered into one of the most easily digested of all starches. In the Caribbean it is used in preference to cornstarch to thicken sauces. Saint Vincent is the source of the majority of the world's supply of arrowroot.

• BANANAS •

Any northerner who journeys to the Caribbean region is astonished at the number of varieties of bananas. In fact, it was only in 1948 that botanists agreed on the origins of this plant, which is really not a tree at all but a large form of grass. At one time, bananas, not apples, were thought to be the fruit of knowledge that Adam and Eve ate in the Garden of Eden.

The banana family ranges in size from tiny delicate ones with slightly sharp taste known as *bananes-figues* in the French-speaking Caribbean to large black-skinned ripe PLANTAINS (see below) that appear fried as *Mofongo* (see Vegetables and Salads) in Puerto Rico. Bananas, because of their form, have always been identified with sexuality. In French Creole the small ones are called "Go get dressed little boy" and the large ones, "Oh, Mama. God help me!"

Bananas are remarkably nutritious and extremely digestible: 100 grams of banana contain as many calories as 100 grams of steak. When ripe, banana starch is changed into sugar. Bananas also contain notable quantities of protein, calcium, and vitamins A and C. They appear in all courses of the meal from appetizing snacks such as Banana Chips (see Appetizers) to desserts such as Bananes Flambées with rum (see Desserts and Sweets), a favorite dish of Napoleon Bonaparte's. A typical Jamaican breakfast consists of boiled green bananas with salted mackerel, and banana jam is a condiment that is enjoyed by some with dishes like roast pork. Banana leaves add an extra fillip to steamed, poached, and baked dishes and give a subtle flavor.

Bananas should be purchased when their skins are unblemished and when they are firm to the touch. They should never be refrigerated.

· BEANS ·

They call them beans; they call them peas; they call them just about everything. What would Caribbean food be without rice and peas (Jamaica), peas and rice (the rest of the English-speaking Caribbean—see Vegetables and Salads), *arroz con gandules* (Puerto Rico), *riz au pois* (Haiti), and *moros y cristianos* (Cuba)? They also appear in soups, stews, and as side dishes.

Historians report that at least ten types of beans were cultivated in slave gardens in the Caribbean in the seventeenth and eighteenth centuries. Some of today's favorite beans in the Caribbean are kidney beans, black beans, turtle beans, red beans, and pink beans. Congo or gunga peas (pigeon peas), also known as *gandules* or gungoo peas, also appear in peas and rice. Black-eyed peas (cowpeas) are less frequently used but do put in an appearance. Culinary anthropologist Maricel E. Presilla, a specialist in the history of Cuban cooking, notes that Cuba's population is divided according to its bean eating habits. The western part of the island including Havana enjoys black beans. The eastern side agrees with its Haitian neighbors and prefers kidney beans (as do Jamaicans).

· BLACK SUGAR   *SEE SUGARCANE* ·

· BOIS D'INDE ·

Some suggest that these are bay rum berries. French sources, though, seem to think that they are just cousins of ALLSPICE.

· BREADFRUIT   *ARTOCARPUS ALTILIS* ·

Captain Bligh of *Bounty* mutiny fame brought the first breadfruit to the Americas. A descendant of breadfruit number one can still be found in the Botanic Gardens of Saint Vincent. The large, round, cannon ball–sized relative of the mulberry provides starch in many Caribbean dishes. Breadfruit is cooked when green or ripe and can be substituted for white potatoes in many recipes. Alternately, it can be thinly sliced and fried as chips, French-fried, or roasted, either in an oven or over an open fire.

Fresh breadfruit can occasionally be obtained in large cities where there is a significant Caribbean population. If so, be sure to look for a globe with no blemishes or soft spots. Frequently, in Caribbean markets, you can buy a part of a breadfruit. If so, purchase what you need, as it will only keep for a few days in the refrigerator.

· BROWN SUGAR *SEE SUGARCANE* ·

· CALABASH *LAGENIA LEUCANTHA* ·

After maturity, the skin on these pumpkinlike gourds hardens and becomes impermeable to water; they are frequently used as cooking utensils in the Caribbean. Dippers, soup bowls, and large service pieces can be found in local markets and make innovative ways of setting the table for a Caribbean meal. Some varieties make it to the table as ingredients for soups and stews. (See CALABAZA below.)

· CALABAZA *CUCURBITA MAXIMA* ·

When you have pumpkin soup in the Caribbean, odds are that the calabaza is the vegetable used. Referred to as pumpkin in the English-speaking Caribbean, *giraumon* or *calebasse* in the French-speaking Caribbean, and West Indian pumpkin in North America, this large yellow-skinned pumpkinlike squash is cut into chunks and added to stews, pureed by nouvelle cuisine chefs, and fried as fritters.

When purchasing, look for a firm and unblemished one with no spots. These can be kept whole for several months in a cool, dry place. As most calabazas are large, they are frequently sold by the piece in Caribbean and Latin American markets. In that case, use them soon after purchase as they will only keep for a few days in the refrigerator. If calabaza is unavailable, use Hubbard or butternut squash in preference to our North American pumpkin.

· CALLALOO *XANTHOSOMA SPECIES* ·

This is the name of a classic Caribbean soup that appears in different guises in various islands (it is even called Pepperpot—see Soups—in Jamaica). It is also the name of the greens that go into the soup. The leaves will frequently take the name calalu (or callaloo) while the roots have a different name entirely. At least two different leaves are called callaloo in the Caribbean. The first is the elephant-ear–shape leaf of the plant that is variously known as dasheen, tannia, yautia, taro, malanga, and *chou Caribe*. The second is better known as Chinese spinach or Indian kale and sometimes called *bhaji,* its Indian name, in Jamaica and Trinidad.

As with most other ingredients, these leafy greens can occasionally be found fresh in Caribbean markets in large cities with a sizable West Indian population. It is also possible to find canned callaloo; Jamaica's Grace brand seems to have the widest distribution. Fresh spinach can be substituted.

· CANE SYRUP ·

This sugar syrup has a hint of the molasses taste of sugarcane. It is used in preparing the Ti-Punch and Punch Vieux (see Beverages) that are the ubiquitous drinks of the French Antilles. A simple sugar syrup is a good substitute.

· CANE VINEGAR ·

A hint of the molasses taste of sugarcane is again the attraction in this white vinegar that is widely used in Jamaica. Substitute distilled white vinegar mixed with a pinch of brown sugar.

· CARAMBOLA *CHRYSOPHYLLUM CAINITO* ·

Called star fruit, or star apple, this multisided fruit becomes a translucent yellow when ripe. Its juice is consumed in the Caribbean and it is frequently found used as garnish or in salads and desserts because of the unusual star shape that it has when sliced.

· CASCADURA ·

Found in Trinidad and Guyana the cascadura or hassah is a type of mudfish similar in taste to shrimp. Cascadura is such a delicacy that it is only the rare visitor to the island who has a chance to sample cascadura curry. The fish can occasionally be found frozen in fish markets in Caribbean neighborhoods. Shelled and cleaned shrimp are an acceptable substitute in cascadura recipes.

· CASSAREEP ·

The juice of boiled-down grated cassava, flavored with brown sugar, cinnamon, cloves, and other ingredients, cassareep is one of the oldest condiments in the Caribbean. It can trace its origins back to the early Indian inhabitants of the region and was discussed in chronicles of the area which date back to Columbus's time. Today, the condiment is mainly found in Guyana and some of the English-speaking islands of the southern Caribbean, where it is used to season Pepper Pot stew (see Main Dishes).

· CASSAVA *MANHIOT ESCULENTA OR BITTER CASSAVA IS ONE VARIETY* ·

Bread made from the flour of this starchy tuber, which is also known as yuca or manioc, was on the menu when Christopher Columbus dined with the king of the Caribe Indians on December 26, 1492. He would have perhaps passed the plate if he had realized that the bitter version of the tuber can be poisonous because of its high percentage of prussic acid, which is dispelled by cooking.

Today the sweet version of the tuber is found in most of the Caribbean and is used to make everything from tapioca to *Pain de Kassav, pan de casabe,* and *Bammie* (see Breads and Baked Goods), the Haitian, Dominican, and Jamaican versions of the same cassava bread that was served to Columbus. Travelers driving down to Port-au-Prince, Haiti, can stock up on the bread at the small town on the outskirts of Cap Haitien where the bread is still baked in the old style over open-air cast-iron griddles. They can also find the bread for sale in the Mercado Modelo in Santo Domingo and in local markets around the region. It can occasionally be found in Caribbean markets in the States. The flour is so emblematic of the region that it has given its name to the French Antillean zouk band, Kassav.

• CHADEC   *CITRUS GRANDIS* •

Chadec is the French name for this fruit, which is also called a shaddock or a pomelo. Thought to be the ancestor of the grapefruit, the fruit is used in marmalades, for juice, and appears candied in local desserts.

• CHANNA •

These are roasted chick-peas, an Indian snack food transplanted to the Caribbean. Channa can be simply salted, flavored with a curry powder mixture, or toasted with a bitingly hot chile covering. Purchased from street vendors, they are nibbled like peanuts in Trinidad and Guyana.

Channa can be purchased in shops selling Caribbean spices or easily prepared at home. (See recipe, page 82.)

• CHAYOTE   *SECHIUM EDULE* •

Also known as christophine, chocho, mirliton, *xuxu,* and vegetable pear, this delicately flavored squash is used in everything from soups to main dishes. The vegetable looks like a light green or whitish pear with a puckered-up mouth at the bottom. It was introduced into the Caribbean from Mexico in the eighteenth century. It is particularly prized in gratins and soufflés in the French-speaking islands. The peel and the seeds of the young chayote are edible. Once the chayote is older, the peel and seeds should be discarded. Chayotes will keep for up to three weeks in the refrigerator.

Chayotes are becoming increasingly available in supermarkets. Look for firm ones with no blemishes. Chayotes can be used in virtually all recipes that call for zucchini, but will produce a more lightly flavored dish.

• CHERIMOYA   *ANNONA CHERIMOLA* •

Sometimes called the custard apple, this fist-sized fruit has a custardlike flesh that tastes like a mixture of vanilla ice cream and banana. Cherimoyas range in color from green to grayish brown to black. They are frequently used as the basis for fabulous tropical ice creams and sorbets.

Cherimoyas should be eaten exactly like Goldilocks' porridge . . . when just right. In the case of the cherimoya, that means when it gives slightly when pressed with a finger and has a characteristically sweetish smell. They are found fresh only in specialty shops and in the subtropical areas of the United States. The rest of us have to content ourselves with canned pulp and juice.

• CHILES *CAPSICUM FRUTESCENS* •

They cross-pollinate with the alacrity of rabbits and have different names wherever you find them. They are called Scotch Bonnet, *Bonda Man'-Jacques, Piment Negresse, wiri wiri,* bird peppers, and more in the Caribbean where they turn up in virtually all courses of the meal except dessert. Seemingly related to the Mexican habanero chile, the lantern-shape chiles of the Caribbean add flavor to the pot as well as heat. If you must make a substitution, be sure that you select a chile with flavor as well. Tabasco sauce, to be used only as a last resort, will add heat, but the subtle flavoring of Caribbean chile will be lost.

In traditional cooking, chiles are always used fresh. No self-respecting rural family would be without its chile bush and many a transplanted Caribbean native has a well-nurtured pot of a favorite chile growing in a sunny kitchen window. I know of one person who has managed to grow Guyanese wiri wiri peppers in Winnepeg, Canada.

Chiles can be purchased fresh in markets selling Caribbean groceries. They are usually found either in baskets or in small packages near the cash register. Look for ones with bright colors and no blemishes. You can have the flavor of the chile and a bit less of the heat if you remove the seeds from the chile before using it. When working with chiles, use rubber gloves or coat your hands with oil to avoid the stinging capsin (the stuff that makes them hot). When you have finished with the chiles, wash your hands thoroughly, as the capsin will seriously irritate your eyes and mucous membranes if it touches them.

• CHOCOLATE *THEOBROMA CACAO* •

Unless you are up on your tropical fruits and vegetables, you'll probably never recognize the cocoa trees growing by the roadside as you drive through the lush Caribbean countryside. You might even miss it in the marketplace on islands like Martinique and Guadeloupe where it appears in two-inch-thick dark brown logs. You *will* recognize it as chocolate when it appears in candy stores as rich truffles and as a flavoring in desserts and sauces.

Log chocolate as it is found in the Caribbean is unavailable in the States. Travelers, though, with culinary interests may want to bring some back if they can find it during their trips to the Caribbean. Bittersweet chocolate is substituted in the recipes in this book.

• **CINNAMON** *CINNAMOMUM VERUM AND ZEYLANICUM CASSIA* •

The rolled up quills of the dried pale-brown inner bark of the cinnamon tree was one of the most precious spices of the ancient Romans. On Caribbean islands like Grenada, it literally grows on trees. Cinnamon is a commonly used spice in the Caribbean along with its coarser, close cousin, cassia *(Cinnamomum cassia)*. When you go into supermarkets in Barbados, the spice shelves do not have cinnamon packages. They simply have packets and boxes labeled spice. The generic term is used only to refer to this specific spice and speaks to the frequency of its use in Caribbean cooking.

Cinnamon is widely available. When purchasing it, look for the quills and not the ground spice, which is usually a mixture of cinnamon, cassia, and Lord knows what else. You can grind your own in a spice grinder or a coffee grinder that is kept for this purpose. You should look for quills that are highly aromatic and keep them in an airtight container so that they do not lose their potency.

• **CLOVE** *EUGENIA CARYOPHYLLATA AND*
SYZYGIUM AROMATICUM •

Cloves, the pink unopened flower buds of a tropical evergreen plant, were one of the spices for which Columbus was searching in 1492. Cloves are indigenous to the Spice Islands of southeast Asia. They arrived in the Caribbean and are now quite at home on a number of islands, notably Grenada, the Caribbean's very own Spice Island.

Cloves are readily available. They should be highly aromatic when purchased and stored in an airtight container. If powdered cloves are needed, grind your own in a spice grinder.

• **COCONUT** *COCOS NUCIFERA* •

For centuries, the coconut palm was virtually the staff of life for the peoples of the Caribbean. From the fronds which were used for roofs, to the logs which were used for houses and rafts, to the rough husk which made rope, the tree provided for many needs. Culinary needs were also well taken care of. Green coconuts provide water that is so pure that it was occasionally used in place of plasma in the South Pacific in World War Two. Coconut oil is the Caribbean cooking oil of choice and the grated meat of the brown ripe coconut appears on the table in all courses from appetizer to dessert.

In northern climes, we've been deprived for years. Today, we occasionally see jelly coconuts (the green fruit whose meat is still a jellylike mass) in Caribbean markets. But unless you've got a friend with a machete, opening them is not an easy prospect. We therefore remain ignorant about the differences between coconut water and coconut milk.

The liquid in a coconut is coconut water. Coconut milk is the liquid of the coconut mixed with the grated coconut meat. To prepare coconut milk, open a brown or dry coconut by heating it in a medium oven for ten minutes. (The coconut will develop "fault" lines.) Remove the coconut and with a hammer break open the coconut along the "fault" lines. Remove the shell, scrape off the brown peel and grate the white coconut meat. (Using a food processor prevents skinned fingers.) Add 1 cup of heated coconut water or 1 cup boiling water to the grated coconut meat and allow the mixture to stand for half an hour. Strain the mixture through cheesecloth, squeezing the pulp to get all of the coconut milk. Alternatively, unsweetened canned coconut milk can be used. If you're preparing a dessert and really desperate, you can dilute coconut cream.

Coconut water can be purchased at Caribbean markets where enterprising folk are setting up stands complete with machetes so that they can open the coconuts for you. (Avoid the canned sweetened Asian type and look for the water straight from the coconut.) Coconut oil is readily available, as is coconut cream, which is frequently used in Caribbean drinks such as the piña colada. And of course there are always the hairy brown coconuts that peer out at us from greengrocers' bins with whimsical faces made from their "eyes." They can be transformed into coconut milk, grated coconut, and just about any other coconut product you may need.

• COLOMBO   *SEE CURRY* •

• CONCH   *STROMBUS GIGAS* •

This large gastropod mollusk abounds in the Caribbean where the shell is used as a horn. (Called Abeng in Jamaica, it was used to signal many a slave revolt.) The large and singularly unattractive inhabitant of the shell is considered a delicacy in the Caribbean and eaten in many guises. The mucilaginous string that attaches the conch to its shell is considered an aphrodisiac in the Bahamas and consumed with gusto by the male patrons who frequent the conch stands under the bridge heading to Nassau's Paradise Island, much to the intestinal distress of those who have come to sample the more palatable Conch Salad (see Appetizers), which is made from chopped conch, raw onion, and bird peppers mixed together and served with a squirt of lime juice. Called *Lambi* (see Main Dishes) in the French-speaking Caribbean, after the Caribe term, they are served in stews and grilled. An amazingly sexist creole proverb says of a wife-beating husband that "*I bat li con lambi*" (He beats her like a conch). It is an unpleasant reminder of the way that conch must be thoroughly beaten to tenderize it before cooking.

• CORIANDER   *CORIANDRUM SATIVUM* •

The leaves of this plant, which is a relative of the carrot family, are also known as Chinese parsley and cilantro. Brought to the New World by the Spaniards, it is still emblematic of the foods of the Spanish-speaking Caribbean. The seed pods and seeds of the plant are used to make several of the West Indian curries.

• COWPEA   *SEE BEANS* •

• CRAPAUD •

This is a French word used to describe the large frogs that can be found on the islands of Montserrat and Dominica. They are also known as mountain chicken and considered a local delicacy.

• CURAÇAO •

The name of one of the islands of the Netherlands Antilles is also the name of a liqueur that is produced on that island. Excellent in cooking and in making mixed drinks with other ingredients and a perfect after-dinner drink in itself, it has spawned many imitators, but true curaçao comes only from Curaçao.

• CURRY •

Transported to the New World from India, this mixture of spices varies from island to island and from dish to dish. Allspice, an unheard-of ingredient in Indian curries, is frequently a prime ingredient in most West Indian curries. Trinidadian curries tend to be fiery hot. Jamaican ones run the gamut of tastes from mild to hot. In the French Antilles, curry is called *colombo,* and such dishes as Colombo de Porc (see Main Dishes) mix India's spices with the New World's favorite meat . . . pork. Curry is the basis of Trinidad and Tobago's favorite street food, *roti,* a chicken, beef, or vegetable curry wrapped in a plain, flat crepelike bread. In Guyana, they eat their curry with roti too. There, though, they tear off pieces of the roti and dip it into the curry in a style closer to that of India.

• DASHEEN   *SEE CALLALOO* •

• DJON-DJON •

These are tiny black mushrooms that are only available in Haiti and are used to add color and flavor to local dishes such as *riz djon-djon,* a Haitian rice and mushroom dish in which the mushrooms are used to flavor the rice and then discarded.

Djon-djon can be found in markets in Haitian neighborhoods. If you cannot find them, you can substitute reconstituted dried dark European or Asian mushrooms for an approximate taste.

• DRIED SHRIMP •

More common in Brazilian dishes, dried smoked shrimp are found in a few Caribbean dishes where they are ground and used to add flavor to rich sauces. Dried shrimp and more pungent dried smoked shrimp can be found in Asian markets.

• EGG POWDER •

This reddish powder is used for flavoring and for adding color to such dishes as Jamaican roast chicken Chinese-style (see Main Dishes). The powder can be purchased at Asian markets and specialty stores.

• GEERA *CUMINUM CYMINUM* •

This is an Indian term for cumin, a spice that appears frequently in the curry powders of the Caribbean.

• GENIPS *ALLOPHYLUS PANICULATA* •

The fruit of the genip tree look for all the world like enormous grapes. Genips, or guineps, however, have a thick slip skin and a small pit surrounded by a translucent pinkish pulp that can be acidy tart or slightly sweet. Sucking the meat off the pit is a Caribbean children's delight. Kids always seem to know where to find genips growing. The rest of us can find this fruit in markets, sold in bunches or clusters. In one of the eternal confusions of the naming of things in the Caribbean, what are called genips in Jamaica is called akee in Trinidad and vice versa.

Genips are very occasionally found in Caribbean markets. Otherwise, this is one you'll have to sample on the spot in the Caribbean.

• GINGER *ZINGIBER OFFICINALE* •

This rhizome of a tropical plant is probably a native of Asia. It has done so well in the New World, though, that Jamaican ginger has become synonymous with the quality spice for many of us. Ginger is used fresh, dried, or powdered in many of the region's recipes, where it turns up in everything from ginger beer to candied ginger and ginger tea. One Jamaican lemonade recipe even calls for a few gratings of peeled fresh ginger to give it some zing.

Ginger can be found fresh in virtually all greengrocers. If purchasing powdered ginger, look for Jamaican ginger, which is more delicate in flavor.

• GUAVA *PSIDIUM GUAJAVA* •

This fruit is native to the Americas; there are over 100 edible varieties. Père Labat, the French priest to whom we owe much of our knowledge of things gastronomic in the seventeenth-century Caribbean, leaves several recipes for guavas including one for baked guavas. A rich source of minerals and vitamins A and C, guavas are eaten at various stages of their development. When green, they are slightly tart; when ripe they are sweeter. In the Caribbean, guavas are eaten in all ways, but more often than not they are used to prepare jams, jellies, and chutneys.

You may find fresh guavas in markets selling Caribbean produce. If so, look for fruit that is firm with no blemishes. If fresh guavas are unavailable, you'll have to content yourself with guava products ranging from guava nectar to preserved guavas to guava paste (see Guava Cheese in Desserts and Sweets), which is eaten with cheese as a dessert on some Spanish-speaking islands.

· HEARTS OF PALM ·

Those swaying palm trees that make Caribbean beaches picture-postcard paradises also leave their culinary offering in the form of reddish-hued palm oil that is a hallmark of Brazilian cooking (but infrequently used in the Caribbean), in jaggery or palm sugar, in the palm wines of West Africa, and in hearts of palm. This is exactly what it sounds like: the heart of a palm tree. It is found fresh in the Caribbean, and if you are fortunate enough to happen across fresh heart of palm, remove the coarse outside husk and boil the heart in water to which you have added a bit of lemon juice, to keep it from discoloring. When the heart is tender, remove it, drain it, and serve it either with a vinaigrette as a salad, in fritters, or with a hollandaise sauce and asparagus.

Fresh hearts of palm are as rare as hen's teeth in northern climes; we have to content ourselves with the canned variety, which is best used in salads.

· IGNAME *MEMBERS OF THE DIOSCOREA FAMILY* ·

Known as the yam, *ñame,* yautia, and tannia in the Caribbean, this large hairy tuber has nothing to do with what we folks in the United States call yams. Yams have flesh that can range in hue from white to purplish, and the largest of them weigh in at a quarter of a ton. For many African nations, yams were a symbol of life's continuation, because new yams grow from older roots. This religious significance continued on to the New World, where new yams are consecrated in voodoo temples in Haiti during a ceremony known as *mangé yam* (yam eating). An astonishing number of different types of yams are sold in the Caribbean, each with its own local name in English, French, Spanish, Dutch, and patois, which makes identifying them a herculean task. If you want to sample some of the variety, head for your local Caribbean market where Roots: The Vegetable Saga can be investigated. Yams are served in a variety of ways in the Caribbean, ranging from boiled and pureed like mashed potatoes to French-fried or cut up and added to soups and stews.

When purchasing yams, look for firm ones with no signs of mold or insects. Larger yams are usually sold in pieces by the pound, and you should look for pieces that are not soft or spongy.

• JACKFRUIT *ARTOCARPUS INTEGRA* •

This fruit is so often confused with its close cousin, the breadfruit, that it has become a bit of a joke to Caribbean folk, who are used to seeing one labeled with the other's name. Introduced to Jamaica at the end of the eighteenth century by Admiral Rodney, it made its way to Hispaniola and from there to the rest of the Caribbean. Less aromatic than its Asian relative the durian, the jackfruit is never eaten raw. The fruit can grow up to seventy pounds in weight and thirty- or forty-pound jackfruits are not uncommon.

• JAMAICA *HIBISCUS SABDARIFFA* •

The deep red flower of the *Hibiscus* family is sometimes known as sorrel or roselle (rosella) and in Spanish as *flor de Jamaica*. The podlike flowers of the plant are dried and then steeped in water to make a brilliant red drink that has the slightly tart taste and the color of cranberry juice. The drink is consumed as a nonalcoholic beverage by children, but becomes another thing altogether with the addition of rum. It is a traditional Christmas drink. Formerly found in Caribbean markets at Christmastime, sorrel is now available almost year-round.

• JAMAICA PEPPER *SEE ALLSPICE* •

• KID •

The meat of young goats is occasionally used in West Indian cookery, most notably in Jamaica's Curry Goat (see Main Dishes) and manish water. The meat has a slightly gamy taste.

Kid is available from butchers in West Indian and in Greek neighborhoods. If you cannot find it, it can easily be replaced with mutton.

• LAMBI *SEE CONCH* •

• LAND CRABS •

These small hard-shelled members of the crab family are not sea dwellers, but rather just what they say: land crabs. They are found strung together in bunches in markets in the Caribbean where they are put in pens and fed a diet of bread and spices. They are the main ingredient in one of the French Antilles' favorite appetizers, Crabes Farcies (see Appetizers). Called *jueyes* in Puerto Rico, they turn up in that island's *empanadillas de jueyes,* a land crab cake that is delicious when served with Green Coconut water (see Beverages) in Loíza Aldea.

The taste of land crab is completely different from that of its water-loving cousin. However, if you must replace land crabs, find and use the smallest, most delicate-tasting sea crabs that you can.

· LANGOSTA ·

Known in the French islands as *langouste* (as opposed to *homard*) and in the English-speaking ones as spiny lobster or simply lobster, langosta is a surprise for many northerners traveling to the region. Unlike its cousins from Maine and New England, the Caribbean lobster has no pincer claws. It makes up for this lack by having some of the tastiest of any lobster meat.

Langosta are occasionally found in specialty fish markets; if you can find them, prepare them according to any of the lobster recipes in this book. If not, you can replace langosta, but not its delicate taste, with regular lobster meat.

· LARD ·

Rendered fatback is known as lard. Lard is frequently found in Puerto Rican recipes where it is known as *manteca de cerdo,* and is readily available in the meat compartments of most grocery stores and supermarkets.

· LÉLÉ ·

A *lélé* or *baton lélé* is a stirring stick used in Caribbean cooking to whisk up such dishes as Callaloo Voodoo (see Soups) or Mignan de Fruit à Pain (a breadfruit puree, see Vegetables and Salads). A *baton lélé* can be purchased inexpensively in any market on Martinique or Guadeloupe, or it can easily be made from a small stick with three or four smaller branches growing from the end which has had the bark peeled off and been dried.

· LIMES *CITRUS AURANTIFOLIA* ·

A member of the Rutaceae family that also includes oranges and lemons, Caribbean limes have yellow skins and look like small green lemons; they only turn yellow when overripe. Limes are the basis for numerous dishes and are prime ingredients in most of the region's drinks, such as rum punch and the Ti-Punches (see Beverages) of the French Antilles. In the French-speaking islands of the region, they are cut *en palettes,* that is, sliced around the center so that each slice is seedless, and served as condiments for everything for callaloo to salads.

Caribbean limes rarely make their way to northern markets. Instead, select the juiciest limes that you can find with no blemishes or soft spots.

· MACE *SEE NUTMEG* ·

• MANGO *MANGIFERA INDICA* •

This tropical fruit par excellence is known by some as "the king of the fruits." Over 326 varieties have been recorded in India, although the fruit is thought to have originated in the Malaysian archipelago. Mangoes arrived in the New World (Brazil) in the fifteenth century and in the Caribbean after 1872. It's difficult to be exact about the year, for in 1872, a French vessel carrying a cargo of mangoes from the Iles Bourbon to Hispaniola was captured by the English off Jamaica, the cargo was jettisoned, then floated to various Caribbean islands where it reproduced. The most common mangoes in the Caribbean are Julie mangoes, which are flattened light green ovals. However, there seem to be different varieties almost daily. In fact, there are so many different types, a catalogue would be difficult.

Mangoes are used in many different ways in the Caribbean. Green mangoes are used in hot sauces and in condiments such as kuchela. Ripe mangoes appear in desserts and candies and even pureed in drinks. Needless to say, to many, a ripe mango simply sucked on or cut open and eaten is one of the delights of the tropics.

Once a hard-to-find specialty fruit, mangoes are becoming more and more readily available in the States and Europe. If you cannot find them at your regular greengrocers', look in shops selling Caribbean and tropical produce. Mangoes should be purchased when they are firm but yield slightly to the touch. A sniff will tell you if they are aromatic.

• MANIOC *SEE CASSAVA* •

• MIRLITON *SEE CHAYOTE* •

• MOLASSES •

Called *mélasse* in French and *melao de caña* in Spanish, this by-product of the refining of sugarcane is a spicy thread that runs through the history of blacks in the New World. Molasses, along with rum, was one of the products of the triangular trade that brought most of the slaves to the New World and was one of the Americas' principal sweeteners until the middle of the nineteenth century. As a result, the dark, spicy taste of molasses can be found in the traditional sweets of the area such as Jamaica's Bustamante's Jawbone and Bullas and Guyana's Christmas Cake (see Breads and Baked Goods)—although many replace the traditional sweetener with brown sugar.

Molasses is easily available right where it's always been, waiting for you at the supermarket near the sugar products. Try using a spoonful instead of sugar in some of your usual dessert recipes.

· ÑAME   SEE IGNAME ·

· NASEBERRY   *LACHRAS ZAPOTA* ·

A native of the Caribbean, this fruit is known as sapodilla or *nispero* in Spanish and *sapotille* in French. The French say that the color of the kiwi-size fruit is the color of the skin of beautiful mulatto women. Indeed, it is a lovely golden brown fruit that has a slightly grainy pulp of honey-brown hue. The Mexican name for the tree is *chicozapote,* and the sap from the tree is known as *chicle,* the substance from which chewing gum is made. Naseberries are usually eaten simply as fruit. Recently, though, they have begun to appear in tropical fruit salads and sorbets.

If selecting a naseberry for eating, look for one that is soft to the touch, but without blemishes. When they are too firm, they are underripe and have an unpleasant sour taste.

· NUTMEG AND MACE   *MYRISTICA FRAGRANS* ·

Two of the spices that Columbus was looking for when he stumbled upon the Caribbean, nutmeg and mace are from the same tree. The nutmeg is the seed and the mace is the lacy aril that covers it. Grenada, the Caribbean's Spice Island, is one of the world's largest producers of nutmeg today, and the tall, tropical evergreen from which the nuts come scents the air with its fragrance. Nutmeg has been a popular spice in Caribbean cooking for centuries: a grating is indispensable to a true rum punch and the grated spice subtly enhances curries, stews, soups, and desserts.

If purchasing nutmeg, forget about the grated stuff in cans or jars. Get a nutmeg grater and whole nuts, which will release a small bit of oil when pressed if they are good quality.

Mace can be found in its natural form, which is called blades. These are good for adding to soups and stews, but for baking and other uses you will have to resort to ground mace. Buy it in small quantities and store it in an airtight container, as it rapidly loses its aroma.

· OKRA   *HIBISCUS ESCULENTUS* ·

This relative of cotton is perhaps one of the least-liked vegetables of the Western world. People just don't like its "slimy" texture. In the Caribbean, they simply let okra be itself and prize the pods for their ability to thicken sauces and soups. Okra is known as *gombo* in France, *quingombo* in Puerto Rico, *malondron* in the Dominican Republic, and sometimes by its East Indian name, *bindi,* in Trinidad and Jamaica. It adds the stick-to-your-ribs quality to Callaloo and to Jamaica's Pepper Pot and turns up in Puerto Rico's sopa de quimbombo (see Soups). It also appears solo as a vegetable and blanched as a salad.

In selecting okra, which is readily available in markets in African-American and Caribbean neighborhoods in the United States, look for small pods that have no blemishes. The smaller pods are more delicate in taste and not fibrous as some of the larger pods. In cooking okra, remember, the more you cut it, the slimier it will be.

• OTAHEITE APPLE *SYZYGIUM MALACCENSE* •

Also known as a pomerac, this fruit looks too good to be true. The pear-shaped fruit has a waxy, burgundy-red skin and pristine white flesh. Eaten mainly as a fruit, it can also be sliced thin to add color and a very subtle taste of apples mixed with roses to salads.

• OURSIN •

This is what islanders on Martinique and Guadeloupe call the small spiny sea urchins, which are no fun if you step on one at the beach. At the dinner table, it's another story, for they are delicious when they appear as appetizers, either baked or raw.

• PAPAYA *CARICA PAPAYA* •

Known as *fruta bomba* in Cuba, *lechosa* in the Dominican Republic and Puerto Rico, *papaye* in the French-speaking Caribbean, and erroneously as pawpaw or melon tree in many English-speaking islands, the papaya is a native of the Caribbean. Papayas can vary in size and look like everything from small, unripe Crenshaw melons to misshapen yellow squashes. The flesh varies in color from light pink to deep orange and even red. When cut open, papayas have a myriad of small black seeds, which are not usually eaten but reputed to have a taste between watercress and pepper. Papaya usually appears on Caribbean tables at breakfast or at dessert, sliced and accompanied by a wedge of lime; they are also eaten green in salads and condiments.

A surprising property of the papaya is that it has a remarkable ability to tenderize meat, thanks to its large quantity of the enzyme papain, which also aids in digestion. Tough pieces of meat are made virtually fork tender by wrapping them in papaya leaves or rubbing them with papaya juice. For this reason, papaya is the basis of many commercial natural meat tenderizers.

Papayas are still not as common in markets as mangoes. However, if you find one, be sure that it is slightly firm to the touch and has no blemishes or soft spots. You can also get canned papaya nectar and other papaya products at specialty shops carrying Latin American and Caribbean products.

• PASSION FRUIT   *PASSIFLORA INCARNATA* •

This fruit from the passionflower can resemble a thick-skinned yellow or purple plum. Inside, numerous small black seeds are encased in a yellow or orange-colored translucent flesh, which is wonderfully tart and almost citrusy. Called *maracudja* in some parts of the French-speaking Caribbean and *granadille* in others, *granadilla* in the Spanish-speaking Caribbean, and passion fruit in the English Caribbean, the fruit is a delight for visitors to the region.

Better known for its juice than in itself, the fruit's tart taste can be found in sorbets and in desserts throughout the region. The juice's distinctive tart taste can be found in numerous liqueurs mixed with everything from rum to Cognac, and in many commercial fruit juices.

Passion fruit is not readily available in the northern United States; however the juice and liqueurs are.

• PEPPER SAUCES •

The Arawaks made several pepper sauces. *Taumalin* was prepared from limes, chiles, and crabmeat. The tradition goes on today with the Caribbean region producing a seemingly infinite variety of pepper sauces. Any hot stuff–loving individual making a trip to the Caribbean should attempt to sample as many sauces as possible because each has its own zing. Jamaica's Pickapeppa sauce has a rich brown coloring and a heartiness somewhat like a peppery Worcestershire sauce. Bellos, from one of the smaller islands, seems to be red liquid fire. Barbados's Bonney Pepper Sauce mixes Scotch Bonnet chiles with a mustardy base. Matouks from Trinidad has a tamarind or papaya base.

As northern taste buds are turning more toward things piquant, Caribbean pepper sauces are becoming more readily available. Head to your local Caribbean market and sample what's there.

• PIGEON PEAS   *CAJANUS CAJAN* •

Called gungoo peas, Congo peas, or *gandules,* these are the peas that frequently go into Rice and Peas (see Vegetables and Salads). Of African origin, this field pea is usually found dried. Fresh ones are occasionally available and can be prepared and eaten like regular garden peas. Pigeon peas are usually found dried or canned in U.S. markets.

• PISQUETTE •

This is one of the names in the French Caribbean (the other is ti-ti-ri) for the small whitebaitlike fish that is prepared in omelettes and fritters, or fried and eaten with gusto. These small fish are found in the mouths of rivers and caught with fine nets. They can be replaced in recipes by whitebait or similar small fish.

· PLANTAIN *MUSA PARADISIACA* ·

This is the big brother of the banana family. Plantains are never eaten raw
and are starchier than bananas. Readily available in markets selling Caribbean and Latin American produce, the ripeness of the plantain determines
its cooking use. Green plantains are suitable for Plantain Chips (see Appetizers) and adding to stews and such because of their high level of
starch. Yellow medium-ripe plantains are good for dishes such as Puerto
Rico's Mofongo (see Vegetables and Salads) as they are soft but still have
not lost their starchy taste. Black-skinned ripe plantains are those where
the starch has turned to sugar. They are perfect for dessert dishes. Green
plantains should be peeled under cold water to avoid staining your hands.

· RICE *ORYZA SATIVA* ·

Although Asia is the continent that immediately comes to mind when rice
is mentioned, some parts of Haiti grow rice in paddies very much like
their Eastern counterparts. The dish is also a major part of many Caribbean meals. . . . What would island cooking be without Rice and Peas
(see Vegetables and Salads)? Rice turns up in Guadeloupe's *colombos,*
Trinidad's curries, and Puerto Rico's *asopaos.*

Several varieties of rice are available in the Caribbean where "pickin' "
rice (removing the impurities and stones from it) is still a necessity. Uncle
Ben's seems to be the rice of preference, but use whatever you're used to.

· RUM ·

Visions of piña coladas and rum punches are immediately conjured up
by the mention of the word "rum" in conjunction with the Caribbean.
Few, though, will remember the tempestuous history of the beverage in
the region. Rum is the distilled spirit made from sugarcane, molasses, or
sugarcane by-products. Columbus is said to have brought the cane to the
Caribbean from the Canary Islands on his second voyage. The plant
thrived, and by the sixteenth century, rum was on its way to becoming a
regional delight. Called Kill Devil and *Guildivel,* the raw spirit was said to
be responsible for Port Royal in Jamaica being the wickedest town in the
world. Rum fueled the British Navy, brought comfort to European planters and slaves alike.

Each Caribbean island produces its own rum. You can tell who lives in
a particular Caribbean neighborhood by looking at the rum shelves of the
local liquor shop. Brugal, Bermudez, and Barcelo and you're guaranteed
a Dominican population. XM or El Dorado and you've found your way to
a Guyanese enclave; Barbancourt, and you're in a Haitian hangout. Puerto
Rico favors Don Q and Bacardi (which originated in Cuba, but is now
located in Puerto Rico); Barbados produces Cockspur and Mount Gay;
Jamaica has Appelton, Myer's, and Wray and Nephew; Martinique fea-

tures Rhum Saint James, Rhum La Negrita, and Rhum Maulny; and Trinidad makes Old Oak. Because these are products of larger distilleries, they are exported to Europe and the States and therefore tend to be among the best known. However, other areas of the region also produce their own rums.

Up until the early twentieth century, many large landowners in the region produced their own rums for their families and friends. These smaller distilleries are the origins of many of the specialty brands today, such as Puerto Rico's Barillito and some of Guadeloupe's *rhum agricole*. Sought after by rum connoisseurs for the individual flavors, these brands, when aged, frequently have many of the characteristics of fine Cognacs.

The lighter Puerto Rican rums are perfect mixers and can also substitute for other liquors. Try a rum Bloody Mary, or a rum and tonic, or a rum and water using the Anejo. Jamaica's Appelton and Myers's rums are the quintessential rum-punch rums. Barbados's Cockspur and Mount Gay are good with mixers like ginger ale, which allow their taste of cane to shine through; that is also true of the rums of Martinique, if you can find them. For an after-dinner treat, try a snifter of twelve-year-old Barbancourt from Haiti.

• SAFFRON *CURCUMA DOMESTICA OR CURCUMA LONGA* •

In the Caribbean, more often than not, what is sold as saffron is really turmeric. This rhizome, which is a relative of ginger, adds color and taste to many of the West Indian curries. It's called *safran-pays* in the French-speaking Caribbean.

If you happen upon a spice basket from Grenada, the small dried root labeled saffron is turmeric and can be grated as needed. If not, most spice shops sell powdered turmeric. Buy small quantities, as the spice keeps its colorant properties indefinitely but loses its flavoring ones rather rapidly. As with all spices, keep the turmeric in a tightly covered container.

• SALTFISH •

While occasionally salted mackerel is available, what is usually referred to as saltfish in the Caribbean is salted codfish. Known as *morue* in the French-speaking islands and as *bacalao* in the Spanish-speaking ones, saltfish is another part of the history of the region: In the days of the Atlantic slave trade, the slave price was paid in Spanish coins, rum, or salted codfish. Because it was easily transported, saltfish was sometimes fed to slaves on the Middle Passage, but it was expensive and did not make a regular appearance.

Up until recent years, saltfish was an inexpensive item in Caribbean households. It is found in dishes throughout the area, such as Jamaica's Stamp and Go (see Appetizers) and ackee and saltfish, in Guadeloupe's calalou, and in Puerto Rico's Bacalaitos (see Appetizers). Times have changed and now it is not uncommon to hear folk complain that saltfish has become so expensive that it is prohibitive for many of the poorer households. Imagine the northerner's amazement at being asked to bring pieces of saltfish down to the Caribbean!

Saltfish is usually readily available in Caribbean markets. Look for pieces with white flesh (yellow flesh indicates age).

To prepare, soak the fish overnight in cold water. Drain, then place in a saucepan and cover with fresh cold water. Bring the water to a boil and simmer for 15 minutes, or until the fish is tender. Skin and flake the fish.

If you are in a hurry and unable to soak the fish overnight, wash it in several changes of cold water, place it in a saucepan, cover it with fresh cold water, bring it quickly to a boil, and drain immediately. Then skin, flake, and proceed with the recipe.

• SAPODILLA   *SEE NASEBERRY* •

• SEASONING •

This is a Barbadian term for the mixture of chives, fresh thyme, and other herbs that is used to season chicken and fish.

• SOFRITO •

This mixture is a seasoning staple in most Puerto Rican kitchens. There are as many variations to the sofrito recipe as there are Puerto Rican grandmothers. Most mixtures contain pork, lard, green peppers, tomatoes, onions, and coriander as main ingredients; they are prepared in advance and stored in the refrigerator, then added to a variety of dishes.

If you don't wish to prepare your own Sofrito (see Sauces, Condiments, and Seasonings), you can purchase it ready-made. Goya produces a variety.

• SORREL   *SEE JAMAICA* •

• SOURSOP   *ANNONA RETICULA* •

This fruit, called *corossol* in the French-speaking Caribbean and *guanabana* in the Spanish-speaking countries, was introduced into the Caribbean region from South America in the sixteenth century. It looks somewhat like an artichoke, but can also have a smooth green or greenish brown skin. The thick skin covers a creamy white fruit that has a sweet, slightly acid flavor. French missionary Père Labat, who left many testimonies to Caribbean gastronomy in the eighteenth century, records a recipe for baked soursop with orange-flower water and cinnamon that still sounds good today. However, the fruit is usually consumed raw or in juices, sorbets, ice creams, and candies in the contemporary Caribbean.

Soursops rarely appear in northern markets, since they don't travel well. However, if you're lucky, select one that is slightly soft to the touch without too many blemishes.

• SPICE •
This is a Barbadian term for cinnamon.

• SUGARCANE   *SACHARUM OFFICINARUM* •
This "honey-bearing reed" was brought to the Caribbean from the Canary Islands by Columbus on his second voyage. The plant grew and thrived, and by the seventeenth century, the Sugar Revolution changed the face of the Caribbean socially, politically, agriculturally, and economically. Small land holdings became outmoded as sugar could only be grown economically on large estates. The arduous task of growing the cane and processing it into sugar, molasses, and rum was the labor of the hundreds of thousands of slaves imported from Africa. These were the glory days of the West Indies when the phrase "as rich as a West Indian planter," indicating great wealth, was heard in the fanciest salons of Great Britain.

Up until recently, we have been removed from true sugar, seeing instead the refined superfine white crystals instead of the intense-tasting real thing. A push to natural foods has instructed us that the unrefined sugar is better for us, and many people, if able, will opt for the cane taste of Moscovado sugar, which is the last sugar left in the barrel after the molasses has been drained off. Brown sugar and the darker black sugar are still available in the Caribbean and a treat for those who get to cook with them. They appear in Jamaica's Bun and in Guyana's Christmas Cake (see Breads and Baked Goods) and in virtually all of the region's baking.

Caribbean sugars are frequently available in shops selling Caribbean products and are relatively easy to obtain. If not, you can substitute dark brown sugar.

• SWEET POTATO   *IPOMOEA BATATAS* •
The confusion between what are yams and what are sweet potatoes still reigns. According to botanists, the yam is a thick, hairy tuber that may have flesh in hues ranging from pristine white to slightly purple. They are all members of the Dioscorea family (see IGNAME). Sweet potatoes grow on a trailing perennial plant and usually have orangey skins and flesh that can range in color from pale white to deep reddish orange. Both yams and sweet potatoes are eaten extensively in the Caribbean. However, there, unlike in the States where sweet potatoes are often erroneously called yams, the confusion does not seem to exist. Sweet potatoes are called *patates douces* in the French-speaking islands and *patatas dulces* in the Spanish-speaking ones.

Sweet potatoes are readily available at all greengrocers, particularly in the fall and winter seasons. When selecting sweet potatoes, look for ones that are firm with no blemishes.

• TAMARIND   *TAMARINDUS INDICA* •

This tropical tree produces a brown pod that is processed into an acidulated pulp used in the Caribbean for flavoring everything from chutneys to guava jelly.

Tamarind can be purchased in shops selling Indian products as well as those selling Caribbean products. It usually comes in the form of a prepared pulp, which can be kept for a week or longer in the refrigerator. Prepared tamarind can also be frozen. Tamarind juice is also available.

• THYME   *THYMUS VULGARIS* •

A relative of the mint family, thyme is frequently used in Caribbean herb mixtures. It appears fresh in Barbadian seasoning and in numerous dishes from the French-speaking Caribbean, and dry in a salt-and-herb mixture from Saint Croix.

Fresh thyme is increasingly available in supermarkets. Dry thyme is readily available and may be substituted.

• TURMERIC   *SEE SAFFRON* •

• UGLI   *CITRUS SP* •

This grapefruit-size fruit isn't ugly at all. It is a cross between a grapefruit, an orange, and a tangerine, often called tangelo. It appears on Caribbean tables as juice and as marmalade, and glazed and dipped in chocolate in candies. Ugli fruit can occasionally be found in supermarkets or at the greengrocers.

• VANILLA   *VANILLA FRAGRANS* •

Native to the Caribbean, this is yet another of the New World's gifts to cooking. The pods of this relative of the orchid develop their deep coloring and taste after a lengthy period of processing. Vanilla is one of the world's master spices and is used in much Caribbean baking. Anyone who has seen the fat, oily vanilla beans in the market in Guadeloupe will never want to buy vanilla extract again, but will instead opt to prepare their own by adding a vanilla bean to a small vial of dark rum for a particularly Caribbean (and delicious) baking addition.

• WIRI WIRI •

This is Guyana's answer to Jamaica's Scotch Bonnet–type chile. Tiny little incendiary cannonballs of heat, these are some of the region's most pungent chiles.

·YAM *SEE IGNAME AND SWEET POTATO* ·

· Z'HABITANT ·

This is the French Antillean name for the large crayfish that is frequently used in creole cooking.

· Z'OISEAUX ·

These are bird peppers in the French Antilles.

· Z'YEUX NOIRS ·

This is the French Antillean term for black-eyed peas (cowpeas).

APPETIZERS

The Queen's Park Savannah is the hub of life in Port of Spain, Trinidad. Every Saturday afternoon as twilight begins to fall and the sky rapidly goes from azure to indigo, small stands are set up around the edge of the park. These brightly painted wooden boxes on wheels or more modern metal contraptions immediately attract crowds of men. The stands are not dispensing winning lottery tickets, they are selling mangrove oysters: small oysters that grow among the roots of the trees in the mangrove swamps. These oysters are tiny and delicious when slurped raw from the stands surrounding the Savannah. They are also reputed to have astonishing aphrodisiac powers.

Caribbean peoples are notorious nibblers. Virtually every street corner in the area's capital cities have small stands selling everything from spicy, salted chick-peas called *channa,* to bits of coconut to sweets of every variety. Some of these Caribbean nibbles are wonderful served either with drinks or before a meal. There is also a Caribbean tradition of fritters and fried tidbits—meat patties, corn sticks, and more—that also enter into the appetizer category. Finally, there are the marinated fruits and vegetables called *souskai* in the French Caribbean.

ACRAS DE MORUE

This is the traditional before-dinner snack in the French-speaking Caribbean. The acras are served hot out of the oil and are accompanied by a Ti-Punch. The slightly salty, invariably peppery taste of the acras are a perfect counterpoint to the smooth molasses taste of the Ti-Punch.

½ POUND SALTED CODFISH,
   FLAKED (SEE PAGE 69)

1 SPRIG FRESH THYME

2 SPRIGS FLAT-LEAF PARSLEY

1 SCALLION, INCLUDING GREEN
   TOP

2 CHIVES

¼ TEASPOON ALLSPICE

½ SCOTCH BONNET—TYPE CHILE

ACRAS BATTER (RECIPE
   FOLLOWS)

CORN OIL FOR FRYING (2 INCHES)

SERVES 6 TO 8   Place the flaked codfish, thyme, parsley, scallion, chives, allspice, and chile in the bowl of a food processor and grind them together into a thick paste. Fold this paste into the acras batter.

Meanwhile, heat 2 inches of corn oil to 350° to 375° in a heavy cast-iron pot or deep fryer. Drop the acras into it by the teaspoonful. Fry until they are light brown, turning once. When done, remove with a slotted spoon and drain on paper towels.

ACRAS BATTER

1 CUP FLOUR

SALT AND FRESHLY GROUND
  BLACK PEPPER TO TASTE

2 EGGS

⅓ CUP MILK

Mix the flour and the seasoning together in a medium-size bowl. Make a well in the middle of the flour mixture and break the eggs into the well one at a time while beating the mixture with a whisk. Continuing to beat, add the milk, and beat until the mixture has become a thick, uniform paste. Cover the bowl with a dampened cloth and allow it to rest for 1 to 4 hours.

Add the desired ingredients into the paste before frying.

ACRAS DE ZIEU NOI'S

Black-eyed peas are the basis for this variation on the acras theme that comes from Martinique. They are traditionally eaten during the Easter season on Good Friday. They are Caribbean relatives of Brazil's *acaraje* and Nigeria's *akkra*.

½ POUND DRIED BLACK-EYED
  PEAS

1 CLOVE GARLIC

1 SCOTCH BONNET-TYPE CHILE

3 TABLESPOONS MILK

CORN OIL FOR FRYING (2 INCHES)

SERVES 6 TO 8   The night before cooking, soak the black-eyed peas in cool water to cover. The following day, shake the beans, picking over them to remove any small stones or hardened ones. Pour off the water and replace it by more cool water. An hour before cooking, rub them between your fingers to take off the skins, which should come off easily. Drain well and place in a food processor with the other ingredients. Grind until the mixture becomes a smooth paste which sticks to a spoon. Transfer to a bowl and whip the mixture for a minute. You may also put the beans in a food mill and combine them with the other ingredients in a bowl. Proceed with the recipe.

    Meanwhile, heat 2 inches of corn oil to 350° to 375° in a heavy cast-iron pot or deep fryer. Drop the acras into the oil, a teaspoonful at a time, being careful not to splash the hot oil on yourself. Do not add too many to the pot at once, as that will lower the temperature of the oil and the acras will be runny. Fry until golden brown, turning once. Remove from the oil with a slotted spoon, drain on paper towels, and serve warm.

STAMP AND GO

Just in case you thought that the English-speaking Caribbean didn't have an entrant in the codfish fritter sweepstakes, here's Jamaica's Stamp and Go. No one is quite sure why these are called Stamp and Go, but an undoubtedly apocryphal story relates that they were so named because they are quickly eaten.

½ POUND SALTED CODFISH,
    FLAKED (SEE PAGE 69)
2 SMALL SCALLIONS, INCLUDING
    GREEN TOPS, MINCED
2 SCOTCH BONNET—TYPE CHILES,
    SEEDED AND MINCED
1 SMALL TOMATO, PEELED,
    SEEDED, AND MINCED

2 CUPS FLOUR
2 TEASPOONS BAKING POWDER
APPROXIMATELY ¼ CUP COLD
    WATER
COCONUT OIL FOR FRYING

SERVES 8 TO 10   In a large bowl, mix the flaked codfish, scallions, chiles, and tomato. Mix in the flour and the baking powder and add enough water to make a soft sticky batter.

    Meanwhile, heat the coconut oil to 350° to 375° in a heavy cast-iron pot or deep fryer. Drop in the fritters by the teaspoonful, a few at a time. Fry until golden brown. Drain on paper towels and serve immediately.

BACALAITOS

These are the Puerto Rican take on the codfish fritter. Available all over Puerto Rico, the island's best are reputed to be found in the town of Loíza Aldea, on the north shore. Savvy folk take the drive from San Juan on weekends to sample bacalaitos and drink rum and coconut water in the huts that are set up.

2 CUPS FLOUR

½ TEASPOON BAKING POWDER

½ POUND SALTED CODFISH, FLAKED (SEE PAGE 69)

2 CLOVES GARLIC, MINCED

1 SCOTCH BONNET—TYPE CHILE, MINCED

SALT AND FRESHLY GROUND BLACK PEPPER TO TASTE

2 CUPS WATER

VEGETABLE OIL FOR FRYING

MAKES ABOUT 2 DOZEN   Mix the flour and baking powder in a bowl and add the flaked codfish, garlic, chile, salt and pepper, and water. Stir well to make sure that the ingredients are well blended.

Heat 2 inches of oil to 350° to 375° in a heavy pot. Drop the bacalaitos by teaspoonsful into the oil, a few at a time. (Too many will lower the oil's temperature and make cooking more difficult.) Drain on paper towels and serve warm as appetizers or with cocktails.

SOUSKAI D'AVOCATS

The term *souskai* comes from the French Caribbean and indicates a way of marinating unripe fruits and vegetables. Souskai are traditionally served with appetizers as spicy tidbits. The most common souskai are prepared from green mangoes. However, the following souskai are made from avocado, which is easier to obtain.

2 RIPE BUT FIRM AVOCADOS

1 CLOVE GARLIC, MINCED

½ TEASPOON SALT

1 SMALL SCOTCH BONNET—TYPE
   CHILE, SEEDED AND COARSELY
   CHOPPED

JUICE OF 2 LIMES

SERVES 4 TO 6   Peel the avocados, remove the pits, and cut the fruit into small cubes.

Place the garlic and salt in a food processor or mortar and pestle and grind into a paste. Add the chile and continue grinding. Finally add the lime juice and mix well.

Pour the marinade over the avocado pieces and allow them to sit for at least 1 hour. Serve with toothpicks along with drinks.

PLANTAIN CHIPS

Plantains, the big brothers of the banana family, are found everywhere in the Caribbean. They turn up as appetizers, as starch vegetables, and as traditional accompaniments to many meat dishes. Plantains are used in all stages of ripeness: from firm and green to ripe yellow to overripe black. These plantain chips are a fine Caribbean alternative to potato chips, perfect for nibbling at home.

3 LARGE GREEN PLANTAINS   SALT TO TASTE

VEGETABLE OIL FOR FRYING

SERVES 6   Peel the green plantains according to the directions in the Glossary and cut them into thin rondels.

In a heavy iron pot or deep fryer, heat 2 inches of oil for frying to 350° to 375°. Drop in the plantain rounds a few at a time and fry until browned and crisp, turning once. When the chips are done, remove from the oil and drain on paper towels. When all of the chips are done, place them in a paper bag with the salt and shake to season them. Serve while warm to accompany drinks.

CHANNA

These crunchy snacks are easy to prepare at home.

1 1-POUND CAN CHICK-PEAS
(GOYA IS A GOOD BRAND.)

SALT AND CAYENNE PEPPER TO
TASTE

SERVES 8 TO 10   Drain the chick-peas and place them on a cookie sheet. Season them with salt and cayenne pepper to taste. Place them in the broiler for 3 to 5 minutes, or until golden brown and crunchy. Serve to accompany drinks.

COCONUT CHIPS

Almost anywhere that you drive along Jamaica's north shore, tall stands of coconut palm trees point their fingers up to the sky. The trees provide shade for swimmers at the beaches in Ocho Rios and Montego Bay, and the coconuts provide many a delight for Caribbean diners. Port Antonio, on Jamaica's northeastern side, is perhaps best known as one of the first places to ship bananas to the States. Errol Flynn lost his heart to the lush land there; his hideaway, Navy Island, has been transformed into a cluster of small bungalows that can be rented by visitors. This is where I first tasted coconut chips, salty bits of broiled coconut. The crisp bits have the flavor of intense coconut macaroons and are perfect nibbles with Caribbean drinks, alcoholic or not.

1 RIPE COCONUT, SHELLED AND   SALT TO TASTE

  PEELED

SERVES 8 TO 10   Open a brown coconut by placing it in a 350° oven and then whacking it soundly with a hammer along its "fault" line. Take out the coconut meat, reserving the water for other uses. Remove the brown rind from the coconut meat and pare the white meat into long, thin strips with a potato peeler or grater.

Place the pieces of coconut on a cookie sheet and brown them under the broiler until they are lightly toasted and crisp, about 5 minutes. Remove and sprinkle them lightly with salt. Serve warm with cocktails or as a snack.

PUERTO RICO

SURULLITOS

Surullitos are small tidbits of fried cornmeal and cheese that are perfect accompaniments for drinks or as snacks.

1 ½ CUPS YELLOW CORNMEAL   VEGETABLE OIL FOR FRYING

½ TEASPOON SALT

1 ¼ CUPS HOT WATER

⅓ CUP GRATED SOFT WHITE

  CHEESE (LIKE MOZZARELLA OR

  QUESO BLANCO)

MAKES 10 SURULLITOS   Mix the cornmeal, salt, and water together in a saucepan. Cook it over low heat, stirring constantly, until it becomes a thick mush. Add the cheese, stir to incorporate it, and allow the mixture to cool. Shape the surullitos into thumb-size pieces.

Heat the oil for frying to 375° in a deep fryer or heavy saucepan. Drop the surullitos into the oil a few at a time and fry until golden brown on each side. Drain and serve hot.

CARIBBEAN
GRAPEFRUIT

Although most of us do not think of the grapefruit as being a fruit that can grow in the tropics, it does wonderfully in the Caribbean. This hot grapefruit is a wonderful way to begin or end a meal. It combines the molasses taste of a good Caribbean rum, the sweetness of brown sugar, and the tang of citrus.

3 LARGE RIPE GRAPEFRUIT

6 TABLESPOONS BROWN SUGAR

6 TABLESPOONS DARK BARBADOS
RUM

SERVES 6   Preheat the broiler. Cut the grapefruit into halves and prepare them for eating, being careful to remove the membrane so that each section slides out onto a spoon. Place the grapefruit halves in a baking pan. Sprinkle 1 tablespoon of sugar and pour 1 tablespoon of rum over each grapefruit half.

Place the grapefruit under the broiler for 5 minutes, or until the sugar has caramelized. Serve hot as an appetizer or dessert.

JANGA

Janga are crayfish that can be found in the rivers of Jamaica. They are caught and peppered and are sometimes sold at pork pits on the north coast alongside the ever-popular Jerked Pork (page 152). Because river crayfish are not easily obtainable, I have substituted medium-size shrimp in this recipe.

2 CUPS DISTILED WHITE VINEGAR

1 SCOTCH BONNET—TYPE CHILE,
   SEEDED

1 CLOVE GARLIC, MINCED

1 SMALL ONION, SLICED

4 ALLSPICE BERRIES, CRUSHED

SALT AND FRESHLY GROUND
   BLACK PEPPER TO TASTE

1 POUND COOKED SHRIMP,
   PEELED AND DEVEINED

SERVES 4 TO 6 In a small nonreactive saucepan, prepare a marinade from all the ingredients except the shrimp. Heat the marinade over a medium flame until it boils.

Place the cleaned shrimp in a crock. Pour the boiling marinade over the shrimp. Cover the crock and store it in the refrigerator for at least 12 hours before serving. Serve chilled.

CONCH SALAD

Say Bahamas and you say conch (pronounced "konk"). The seashells from these mollusks are prime souvenirs and displayed for sale on car tops. Conch pearls are rare and appear in gold jewelry and, of course, the meat appears on virtually every menu. Conch aficionados on Nassau will head immediately for the bridge to Paradise Island where they will savor their favorite delicacy fresh out of the shell, still redolent of the sea.

Conch, a large, tough relative of the snail family, must be tenderized before eating (page 57). If you don't have access to fresh conch, or strong arms, canned conch is ready to cook. The salad is made on the same principle as Latin America's ceviche: The chemical reaction between the lemon juice and the conch "cooks" the mixture.

2 CUPS MINCED CONCH MEAT

½ CUP MINCED CELERY

⅓ CUP MINCED ONION

1 CUP PEELED, SEEDED, MINCED
  TOMATO

JUICE OF 1 LEMON

JUICE OF 1 LIME

SALT TO TASTE

½ SCOTCH BONNET—TYPE CHILE,
  MINCED

PARSLEY FOR GARNISH

SERVES 4 Mix all the ingredients (except garnish) together in a large salad bowl. Cover with foil or plastic wrap and allow to sit for 30 minutes. Stir the salad a few times while it sits. Serve in small cups or over a bed of lettuce. For those who prefer their conch salad without the zip of chile, the pepper can be de-ribbed and seeded, or left out. Garnish with parsley.

CRABES FARCIES

At weddings, baptisms, and festivities on Martinique and Guadeloupe, visitors can see women in the traditional Creole dress: Madras head scarf tied in an endless array of variations; multihued Madras or floral satin skirts over intricate petticoats of lace eyelet; and gold jewelry hanging from earlobes, necks, arms, fingers, and even head scarves. The most coquettish and glamorous of these women are known as *matadores* in Martinique, and it is they who have given their name to a restaurant in Pointe du Bout, where traditional Creole specialties are the hallmarks of the kitchen. No creole meal would be complete without a beginning ti-punch or two, some fluffy light acras, and some *crabes farcies,* stuffed land crabs. As land crabs are difficult to obtain in many places, this recipe has been adapted to use small hard-shelled crabs.

JUICE OF 4 LIMES

1 BOUQUET GARNI: 2 CHIVES, 1
   BRANCH FRESH THYME OR ¼
   TEASPOON DRIED, 2 BRANCHES
   FLAT-LEAF PARSLEY

1 SCOTCH BONNET—TYPE CHILE

12 SMALL CRABS

¾ CUP DRIED FRENCH BREAD
   CRUMBS

¼ CUP COCONUT MILK

4 CHIVES, MINCED

1 CLOVE GARLIC, MINCED

SALT AND FRESHLY GROUND
   BLACK PEPPER TO TASTE

3 TABLESPOONS UNSALTED
   BUTTER

MAKES 10 CRABS   Bring to a boil a large pot of water, lime juice, bouquet garni, and half the chile. Scrub the crabs with a brush and drop them, one at a time, into the pot of boiling water. Boil for 20 minutes; remove them, and reserve ½ cup of the cooking water.

Remove the meat from the crab shells and claws, keeping 10 of the shells intact. Mince the crabmeat. Soak the bread crumbs in the coconut milk; mince the remaining ½ chile. Place the crabmeat, milk-soaked bread crumbs, minced chives and garlic, minced chile, and 2 tablespoons of the reserved cooking water into a skillet and cook the mixture lightly over low heat for 10 minutes. Taste and adjust the seasoning and then fill 10 of the crab shells with the mixture. Place a dot of butter on top of each and place them into a 425° oven for 10 minutes. Serve hot.

MANGROVE OYSTERS

You may not be able to line up on the Queen's Park Savannah with the rest of the folk at the mangrove oyster stands. However, if you should find some, they are best savored raw. Open them and serve them on a bed of crushed ice accompanied by lime sections, which should be squeezed over them. The traditional accompaniment is brown bread and butter. If you are not fortunate enough to find mangrove oysters, select the smallest variety you can find. Folks can eat at least six at a time and connoisseurs have been known to slurp up several dozen at a sitting. Plan according to your guests and their tastes.

CONKIES

Conkies is a traditional Bajan dish that is thought to be a descendant of Ghana's Kenkey. Conkies can be either sweet or savory and can be made with everything from grated fresh corn to plantains. When made with corn or cornmeal, they are also called Dunkanoo (page 220). This version is prepared with plantains.

3 RIPE PLANTAINS

2 TABLESPOONS BUTTER

½ CUP BROWN SUGAR

¼ TEASPOON GRATED NUTMEG

½ TEASPOON GROUND CINNAMON

2 TABLESPOONS SIFTED FLOUR

BANANA LEAVES OR ALUMINUM

FOIL

MAKES 1 DOZEN   Place the plantains in a pot of salted water and boil them until they are tender. In a bowl, mash the plantains with a fork and add the butter, sugar, and spices. If necessary, add a little flour to make a thick paste.

Wash the banana leaves and make them pliable by boiling them. Cut the leaves into pieces about 6 inches square. Then drop 2 tablespoonsful of the plantain mixture onto each piece of leaf, roll it up, fold it over, and tie the ends.

Fill a large heavy saucepan with water and bring it to a boil. Add the conkie packages and boil them for 45 to 50 minutes. Serve warm.

PUERTO RICO

CHICHARRÓN

I first learned to eat what my family pronounced "chick-a-roons" from my uncle Jim; these rapidly became one of my father's favorite snacks. Imagine my surprise when I discovered that my chick-a-roons were none other than *chicharrones*, a culinary specialty of the Puerto Rican town of Bayamón. Driving through the town you see small stands with large, curly, crispy lengths of this fried pork rind. The pork rind is weighed out and wrapped in brown paper, which immediately becomes greasy; it is up to you to break the skin down into small bite-size pieces. This is not a snack for those watching their cholesterol. But for those who can indulge occasionally, it is a treat. It is also broken into small pieces and included in Mofongo (page 130).

1 POUND PORK SKIN

¼ CUP VEGETABLE OIL FOR

  FRYING

SALT TO TASTE

Clean the pork skin thoroughly, singeing off any small hairs that may remain. Heat the oil in a heavy skillet or Dutch oven. Cut the pork skin into small bite-size pieces and fry until crisp. Drain on paper towels and salt to taste. Serve slightly warm.

SOUPS

It was deep green and mossy, the color of the light filtering through the breadfruit trees in the nearby forests. The consistency was soupy, but the okra and greens combined to give it a thickness that made it like eating liquid velvet. This was callaloo, which in some ways is the essence of Caribbean cooking. Callaloo may have its origins in the *sauces feuilles* of the West African coast, which combine greens, meat, and okra for hearty stews. In the New World it is eaten as *caruru* in Brazil and as *gumbo z'herbes* in New Orleans. Virtually every Caribbean island has its own variation of callaloo: In Jamaica, what is called callaloo elsewhere is known as pepperpot. The French Antilles call this soup calalou and serve it with a traditional garnish of flaked codfish called *chiquetaille de morue.* In Puerto Rico, this soup is known as *sopa de quingombo,* while in the Dominican Republic, it's known as *merejena.* Its close cousin, *giambo,* is found in the islands of the Netherlands Antilles.

Callaloo should ideally be savored along with good conversation in someone's home. Alternatively, it should be relished in a very special restaurant, such as Chez Clara in Guadeloupe, seated at an outdoor table under the bougainvillea.

CALALOU CHEZ CLARA

Chez Clara is a small seaside restaurant located in northern Basse-Terre. The Clara is Clara Lesueur, a charming Guadeloupean who, upon returning from a modeling career in France, decided to purvey such specialties as calalou. The calalou, which follows several ti-punches and precedes a meal that is likely to include such delicacies as ray with a green-tinged curry sauce, fricasseed conch, and grilled swordfish shish kebab, is a perfect start. Its mossy green hue reflects the lushness of the forests, while its taste reminds the diner of the proximity of the sea. The okra speaks of Africa while the salted codfish reminds of colder climates. In short, the soup is the Caribbean in microcosm.

1 POUND FRESH SPINACH OR
   CALLALOO GREENS

1 POUND OKRA, TOPPED AND
   TAILED

1 MEDIUM-SIZE ONION, COARSELY
   CHOPPED

1 BOUQUET GARNI: SCALLIONS,
   FRESH THYME, AND PARSLEY

SALT AND FRESHLY GROUND
   BLACK PEPPER TO TASTE

½ SCOTCH BONNET—TYPE CHILE,
   MINCED

6½ CUPS WATER

1 CLOVE GARLIC, MINCED

½ POUND COOKED HAM, CUT INTO
   ¼-INCH DICE

JUICE OF 3 LIMES

SERVES 4   Clean the spinach or callaloo thoroughly, and remove the woody central stems. Chop the okra and the callaloo and place them in a large saucepan. Add the onion, bouquet garni, salt and black pepper, chile, and water. Bring to a boil and cook, covered, over a medium flame for 30 minutes. Remove the mixture from the heat and put it through a food mill until it is a smooth puree. Replace it in the saucepan and add the garlic, ham, and lime juice. Continue to cook over medium low heat for 10 minutes. *Do not allow the soup to come to a second boil or it will lose its texture.* Serve immediately.

SOPA DE QUINGOMBO

I first tasted sopa de quingombo in a very fancy French restaurant in the Caribe Hilton in San Juan. The setting was lavish, the rest of the meal was elegant and continental, but the only memory that remains is the incredible taste of the soup, which seemed to bring with it hints of African drums. *Quingombo* means "okra" in Puerto Rico's Spanish; later, I would learn that the word comes almost verbatim from the Bantu word *quingombo,* which also means okra. Then, all I knew was that the soup was ambrosial: rich and not too filling and flavorful.

¼ POUND SALT PORK, CUT INTO
   1-INCH PIECES

1 POUND OKRA, WASHED, TOPPED
   AND TAILED, AND CUT INTO
   PIECES IF LARGE

2 QUARTS COLD WATER

2 MEDIUM-SIZE ONIONS

2 TABLESPOONS SOFRITO (PAGE
   120, OR GOYA MAKES A GOOD
   READY-MADE VERSION)

1 BAY LEAF, CRUSHED

1 TEASPOON MINCED SCOTCH
   BONNET—TYPE CHILE

1 TABLESPOON BUTTER

SALT AND FRESHLY GROUND
   BLACK PEPPER TO TASTE

1 RIPE AVOCADO, HALVED AND
   PITTED

LEMON WEDGES FOR GARNISH

SERVES 6 TO 8　　Place the salt pork in a bowl, cover it with some water, and soak it for 30 minutes. Pour off the water and place the salt pork in a stockpot or large saucepan and cook over medium heat until the salt pork begins to render some of its fat. Place the okra into the pot. Add the cold water, lower the heat, and cook until the pork is cooked and tender.

Place the onions, sofrito, bay leaf, and chile in a food processor or blender and mix until they have become a thick paste. Heat the butter in a skillet and fry the onion-seasoning mixture for 5 minutes. Gradually add ¼ cup of the broth from the okra and salt pork, stirring constantly. Pour the contents of the skillet into the stockpot, stirring to make sure that all of the flavors are well mixed. Continue to heat for 5 minutes. Season with salt and pepper.

Prepare small balls of avocado with a melon baller. Then dish the soup into serving bowls. Add a few avocado balls to each bowl and serve with a wedge of lemon. The lemon is squeezed into the soup by each individual diner.

CALLALOO VOODOO

Callaloo seems to transform itself with the culinary tradition of each island. In the English-speaking Caribbean, callaloo is a hearty soup with an almost stick-to-the-ribs consistency. This was how I first tasted it in Tobago's capital, Scarborough, in a restaurant named Voodoo.

2 POUNDS FRESH CRABMEAT

3 TABLESPOONS PEANUT OIL

3 SCALLIONS, INCLUDING THE
GREEN TOPS, MINCED

2 CLOVES GARLIC, MINCED

2 BRANCHES FRESH THYME,
CRUMBLED, OR ½ TEASPOON
DRIED

½ POUND SLAB BACON, CUT INTO
¼-INCH DICE

1 POUND FRESH SPINACH OR
CALLALOO GREENS, CLEANED
WITH STEMS REMOVED

1 POUND OKRA, TOPPED, TAILED,
AND CUT INTO ROUNDS

7 CUPS WATER

SALT AND FRESHLY GROUND
BLACK PEPPER

1 SCOTCH BONNET—TYPE CHILE,
PRICKED WITH A FORK

JUICE OF 3 LIMES

SERVES 4 TO 6   Brown the crabmeat in the oil with the scallions, 1 teaspoon of the garlic, and the crumbled thyme.

In a stockpot, brown the diced bacon. Wilt the spinach in the rendered bacon fat. Add the okra, cover with the water, and add salt and freshly ground black pepper to taste. Cook for 20 minutes, stirring constantly with a *baton lélé* (see Glossary) or a whisk. When done, add the crabmeat, remaining garlic, and chile that has been pricked with a fork. Continue to cook over low heat for 20 minutes, stirring occasionally. When done, add the lime juice, whisk it through thoroughly, and serve hot.

BAHAMAS CONCH CHOWDER

The conch is considered to be almost all things to folks in the Bahamas. Known locally as hurricane ham, it turns up in everything from salads to main dishes to appetizers to . . . well . . . soups. This chowder can be dressed up for fancy company with a shot of dark rum.

¾ POUND FRESH CONCH MEAT, CLEANED AND TENDERIZED, OR ¾ POUND CANNED

JUICE OF 2 LIMES

3 SLICES BACON, CUT INTO 1-INCH PIECES

1 LARGE ONION, MINCED

1 GREEN BELL PEPPER, MINCED

2 STALKS CELERY, MINCED

2 CARROTS, DICED

1 LARGE BOILING POTATO, DICED

3 LARGE TOMATOES, PEELED, SEEDED, AND COARSELY CHOPPED

4 CUPS WATER

1 BAY LEAF

1 BRANCH FRESH THYME OR ¼ TEASPOON DRIED

1 SHOT DARK RUM

PEPPER RUM (PAGE 110) TO TASTE

SERVES 4 TO 6   Clean the fresh conch meat with the lime juice and then cut the tenderized conch into ½-inch pieces. If using canned conch: wash, cut into pieces, and cook for 10 minutes. Place the conch in a saucepan, cover it with water, bring to a boil, lower the heat, and cook for 20 minutes over low heat. Canned conch will only need 10 minutes. Drain the conch, reserving the cooking liquid.

While the conch is cooking, place the bacon slices in a skillet and cook them until the fat has been rendered. Sauté the onion, bell pepper, celery, carrots, and potato in the oil for 10 minutes. Place the boiled conch, sautéed vegetables, and bacon into a large saucepan or stockpot, add the tomatoes, 2 cups of the reserved conch cooking liquid, water, bay leaf, and thyme and cook for 1 hour. Just prior to serving, taste and adjust the seasonings and add a shot of dark rum to the pot, if desired. Serve hot. Place a cruet of pepper rum on the table and allow each diner to spice up his or her chowder to taste with a dash of the peppery liquid.

SOUPE AUX POIS
ROUGES

Haiti and Cuba, its neighbor to the north, share a love of kidney beans. However, while Cuba's Sopa de Frijol Negro (see following recipe) is well known in the Caribbean culinary lexicon, Haiti's soupe aux pois rouges has yet to be discovered. It is not a refined soup but rather hearty peasant fare. This version is dressed up for a party and includes a dash of dark Haitian rum.

1 POUND KIDNEY BEANS

2 QUARTS WATER

¼ POUND SALT PORK, DICED

1 CUP FINELY CHOPPED
   SCALLIONS, INCLUDING THE
   GREEN TOPS

2 SPRIGS PARSLEY, MINCED

2 SPRIGS FRESH THYME, MINCED

1 BAY LEAF, CRUSHED

1 STALK CELERY, MINCED

1 TEASPOON SCOTCH BONNET—
   TYPE CHILE

SALT AND FRESHLY GROUND
   BLACK PEPPER TO TASTE

1 CUP HOT WATER

6 INDIVIDUAL SHOTS DARK
   HAITIAN RUM

SERVES 6   Pick over the beans, wash them, and put them into a large saucepan or stockpot. Add the water and other ingredients, except the rum. Cover and bring to a boil. Then lower the heat, and simmer for 2½ to 3 hours, until the beans are very tender. Puree the soup in a food processor or put it through a food mill. Taste and adjust the seasonings and return the soup to the pot, adding up to 1 cup hot water to bring the soup to a thick, but not pasty, consistency and serve hot. At each place, serve a cordial glass of dark Haitian rum, which the diners should add to their soup before tasting it.

SOPA DE FRIJOL NEGRO

Cuba, the largest of the Caribbean islands, has a long and fascinating culinary history. The one dish that is perhaps most closely associated with Cuba in the minds of many is black bean soup. The rich soup is hearty enough to be a meal when served with a dollop of rice, a shaving of onion, and a tot of rum. Yet it can be an elegant opener for the fanciest meal when served in thin china bowls. One spoonful and the history of the Caribbean speaks to the taste buds: the beans brought by the African slaves, the chiles that were loved by the Caribs, and the rum that is a remembrance of glory days.

1 POUND DRIED BLACK BEANS

2 QUARTS COLD WATER

2 CUPS COARSELY CHOPPED
  ONION

½ CUP COARSELY CHOPPED
  SCALLIONS, INCLUDING GREEN
  TOPS

3 MEDIUM-SIZE CLOVES GARLIC,
  MINCED

1 SMOKED HAM HOCK

2 BAY LEAVES, CRUMBLED

SALT TO TASTE

1 TEASPOON FRESHLY GROUND
  BLACK PEPPER

½ SCOTCH BONNET—TYPE CHILE,
  SEEDED

½ CUP DARK RUM

SERVES 6   Pick over the beans, rinse them, and put them in a large heavy pot with the water. Cover the pot and bring the water quickly to a boil. Stir the beans, remove them from the heat, and allow them to sit for 1 hour.

When the beans have softened, return the pot to the heat, adding more boiling water if necessary. Then add the remaining ingredients, with the exception of the rum. Continue to cook, covered, over low heat for several hours, until the beans are very tender and the ham falls off its bone. Remove from the heat and remove the ham hock bone and meat. Dice the meat finely and discard the bone. Press the remaining ingredients through a food mill, taste for seasoning, and add the diced ham. At this point, the soup can rest overnight in the refrigerator so that the flavors mingle, or it can be served at once.

To serve, reheat the soup for 5 minutes while stirring in the rum. Side dishes of lemon wedges, cooked white rice, minced onion, or chopped hard-boiled eggs can be served as garnishes.

SOUPE DE GIRAUMON
LE RÉCIF

Le Récif is a restaurant specializing in seafood on one of the main roads from Port-au-Prince to the suburb of Pétionville. Even though specialties are fish dishes, the pumpkin soup with floating pasta bits is a perfect first course for a light lunch. The *giraumon*, or cooking pumpkin, is called *calabaza* in Spanish and is better known by this name in U.S. markets. If it is not available, butternut or Hubbard squash may be substituted.

½ POUND SALT PORK, CUT INTO 1-
   INCH PIECES

1 ½ POUNDS BEEF SOUP MEAT

6 CUPS WATER

2 POUNDS CALABAZA, PEELED
   AND CUT INTO PIECES

2 SCALLIONS, INCLUDING THE
   GREEN TOPS, CHOPPED

1 SHALLOT, MINCED

2 CHIVES, MINCED

1 SCOTCH BONNET—TYPE CHILE,
   PRICKED WITH A FORK

½ CUP COOKED SPAGHETTI, CUT
   INTO PIECES

SERVES 6   Place the salt pork in a large saucepan and cook it over medium heat until it renders its fat and begins to brown. Add the soup meat and brown it in the rendered fat. Add the water and bring the contents of the pot to a boil. Lower the heat and cook for about 45 minutes, or until the meat is tender. Add the calabaza and the remaining ingredients except the pasta and cook until they have completely disintegrated. Check seasonings and add the spaghetti. Cook until the spaghetti is heated through, stirring to make sure that the soup is well mixed. Serve hot in bowls.

CHILLED PEAR SOUP

Pear is the way that many Jamaicans refer to avocados or alligator pears. In fact, the usage is so common that a Jamaican friend asked me once to bring back a European pear so that she would be able to show her helper that there really was another kind of pear. This, then, is chilled avocado soup to the rest of the world, but in Jamaica it's chilled pear.

2 RIPE AVOCADOS

1 QUART CHICKEN BROTH

2 TABLESPOONS FRESHLY
  SQUEEZED LIME JUICE

½ TEASPOON MINCED SCOTCH
  BONNET—TYPE CHILE

SALT AND FRESHLY GROUND
  BLACK PEPPER TO TASTE

MINCED FRESH CHIVES FOR
  GARNISH

DICED AVOCADO FOR GARNISH

SERVES 6   Peel and pit the avocados, then puree them in a food processor or food mill. Add the avocado puree to the chicken broth, stirring well. Add the remaining ingredients except garnishes, mix thoroughly, and chill in the refrigerator for at least 1 hour before serving.

Garnish with freshly minced chives and diced avocado. Serve cold.

CREAM OF BANANA
SOUP

Bananas are all around if you live in the Caribbean. It's no surprise, therefore, that Caribbean cooks use them in everything from soups to desserts. This creamy banana soup with a hint of chile is a perfect way to begin a formal Caribbean meal.

4 OVERRIPE BANANAS

1 TEASPOON MINCED SCOTCH
   BONNET—TYPE CHILE

1 CUP CHICKEN STOCK

2 CUPS WATER

1 CUP HEAVY CREAM

CURLICUES OF RED AND YELLOW
   BELL PEPPER FOR GARNISH

SERVES 4   Peel the bananas and cut them into pieces. Put the bananas and the chile through a food mill until pureed. Place the banana-chile puree, chicken stock, and water in a saucepan and cook for 10 minutes, stirring occasionally. Add the heavy cream, bring to a boil, and remove from the heat.

Serve hot with the curlicues of red and yellow bell pepper for garnish.

COW FOOT SOUP

Culinary anthropologists can find out all types of interesting things from the diets of various cultures. Anyone studying the Caribbean for long will find it hard not to think that Caribbean men are particularly concerned with potency in matters sexual. The region is rife with recipes for restoratives, tonics, and just plain old aphrodisiacs. Cow foot soup is one such recipe. Some Jamaicans swear by it. I make no claims.

3 QUARTS SALTED WATER

1 COW TROTTER, CLEANED AND
   CUT UP

½ SCOTCH BONNET—TYPE CHILE,
   MINCED

1 MEDIUM-SIZE ONION, DICED

1 STALK CELERY, DICED

1 CARROT, DICED

1 SMALL PURPLE TURNIP, DICED

1 CUP PEELED, DICED CALABAZA
   OR BUTTERNUT SQUASH

1 PARSNIP, DICED

½ TABLESPOON SAGO (SEE NOTE)

1 TEASPOON CHOPPED FRESH
   PARSLEY

1 TABLESPOON FRESHLY
   SQUEEZED LIME JUICE

SALT AND FRESHLY GROUND
   BLACK PEPPER TO TASTE

DASH OF GRATED NUTMEG

SERVES 8 TO 10   Put the salted water into a large stockpot and bring it to a boil. When boiling, add the cleaned cow trotter. Bring to a second boil, skim off the scum, and add the chile. Lower the heat and simmer gently for 6 to 7 hours. Take out the cow trotter, remove the meat from the bone, cut it into bite-size pieces, and return it to the stockpot. Add the vegetables and the sago. Bring the soup to a boil again, lower the heat, and cook until the vegetables are tender, about 30 minutes. Add the parsley, lime juice, and nutmeg just before serving.

NOTE ● *Sago is a dry starch, usually from the sago palm tree, used as a thickening agent in cooking. You can buy it at vegetable markets in Caribbean neighborhoods. Alternatively, you can use 2 teaspoons cornstarch.*

PINEAPPLE CONSOMMÉ

While most of us think of the pineapple as coming from Hawaii, it is really a native of Central America and the Caribbean. Its name comes from its resemblance to the northern pine cone. In colonial times, the pineapple became the symbol of hospitality in the Caribbean. Pineapple finials decorated heavy mahogany furniture and were carved in stone gateposts to welcome travelers. The Antiguan coat of arms even boasts a pineapple, the Antiguan Black. This consommé blends chicken broth with fresh pineapple juice and pineapple chunks for an interesting first course.

3 CUPS CHICKEN BROTH   **1** CUP WATER

2 CUPS FRESH PINEAPPLE JUICE ½ CUP DICED FRESH PINEAPPLE

SERVES 4 Blend the chicken broth, pineapple juice, and water together in a saucepan and cook over low heat for 5 minutes. Ladle the soup into bowls in which you have placed 2 tablespoons of diced fresh pineapple. Serve immediately.

PEPPERPOT SOUP

Pepperpot is a soup with as many guises as there are islands in the Caribbean. A stew in Guyana, Trinidad, and Tobago, it is prepared with cassareep, a condiment prepared from bitter cassava that dates back to the Amerindians. In Jamaica, what is called callaloo in the southern Caribbean is known as pepperpot. The dish appears as a hearty vegetable soup in Antigua. It is this version we present, courtesy of Sandra Taylor, who found it while enjoying that island's annual Race Week festivities.

1 POUND EGGPLANT, CUT INTO ½-INCH DICE

½ POUND SPINACH, SHREDDED

½ POUND CALLALOO SHREDDED (PAGE 52)

12 OKRA PODS, TOPPED, TAILED, AND CUT INTO ½-INCH PIECES

1 POUND YAMS, PEELED AND CUT INTO ½-INCH DICE

1 POUND CALABAZA OR BUTTERNUT SQUASH, PEELED AND CUT INTO ½-INCH DICE

2 SCALLIONS, INCLUDING GREEN TOPS, CUT INTO 1-INCH PIECES

2 ONIONS, COARSELY CHOPPED

3 SMALL YELLOW SQUASH, CUT INTO ½-INCH DICE

6 CARROTS, CUT INTO 1-INCH PIECES

½ POUND SALT BEEF (SEE NOTE)

½ POUND PIG'S FEET, CLEANED, SPLIT

5 CUPS WATER

3 CUPS COCONUT MILK

4 CLOVES

2 SMALL CLOVES GARLIC, MINCED

2 TEASPOONS MINCED CHIVES

½ TEASPOON FRESH THYME, CRUMBLED, OR ¼ TEASPOON DRIED

2 CUPS FRESH GREEN PEAS OR FROZEN, DEFROSTED AND DRAINED

¼ CUP TOMATO PASTE

1 SMALL SCOTCH BONNET—TYPE CHILE, PRICKED WITH A FORK

SALT AND FRESHLY GROUND BLACK PEPPER TO TASTE

SERVES 8 TO 10   Place all of the vegetables except the peas in a large stew pot with the meat and the water. Boil until the meat is tender (about 1 hour). Take the pig's feet from the pot and pick the meat from the bones. Return the meat to the pot and add the coconut milk, cloves, garlic, chives, and thyme. After the liquid has resumed boiling, add the peas, tomato paste, and the pricked chile. Simmer the mixture for about 1 hour, or until thick. Adjust the seasoning and serve hot.

NOTE • *Salt beef can be found at butcher shops in Caribbean neighborhoods. If unavailable, you may substitute slab bacon cut into ½ inch dice.*

CHILLED CONSOMMÉ
WITH GINGER

This is a super-quick summer first course that pays homage to Jamaica's ginger.

1 QUART BEEF CONSOMMÉ

2 TEASPOONS GRATED FRESH
  GINGER

1 TABLESPOON DARK JAMAICA
  RUM

JUICE OF 1 LEMON

LEMON PEEL AS GARNISH

SERVES 4   Mix the consommé, ginger, and dark Jamaican rum together in a saucepan and heat for 5 minutes. Add the freshly squeezed lemon juice and chill for 30 minutes. Serve chilled over ice in stemmed glasses, garnished with lemon peel.

SAUCES,

CONDIMENTS,

AND

SEASONINGS

Grenada's Georgetown market is a delight for photographer and food lover alike. Outdoor stands and indoor stalls boast everything from ackee to yam. For any lover of spicy foods, though, the best stalls are the ones selling small pint-sized jars of the turmeric-hued pepper sauce that the ladies bottle and sell. These pepper sauces, bottled individually and without preservatives or ingredients labels, are some of the best that the Caribbean has to offer. They can be light with only a hint of yellow color, deep mustardy saffron, or fiery red and heavy with papaya and tamarind pulp.

Here in the Caribbean, prepared pepper sauces are really only for the lazy, since the ingredients for homemade sauces are close at hand. Some stands sell glistening red, brilliant yellow, and acid green chiles. Alongside these are the tiny bird peppers, which many a Caribbean housewife grows in a pot on the kitchen windowsill, and the little red fireballs known as wiri wiri peppers in Guyana. Any of these chiles, when combined with ingredients ranging from rum to papaya pulp, can make a pepper sauce.

The local taste for chile doesn't stop there. There are also hot chutneys, spicy pickles, even hot peanut butter, and a wide array of accompaniments that find their way to the table to add spice to the Caribbean's culinary life.

SHERRY PEPPERS

Sherry peppers are a Bermudian fact of life. They are a necessary addition to Bermuda's fish chowder, and many Bermudians feel that almost any dish can be enhanced by the subtle mixture of hot chile and aromatic sherry. While those journeying to Bermuda may stock up on a supply of Outerbridges Original Sherry Pepper Sauce, sherry peppers are simple to prepare at home. They also make perfect hostess and holiday gifts, particularly when prepared in antique cut glass and silver cruets. The sherry that is dispensed from the cruet in small dashes is referred to as pepper wine in Barbados.

¼ CUP BIRD PEPPERS   1 ¼ CUPS AMONTILLADO SHERRY.

MAKES 1½ CUPS   Sterilize a stoppered bottle or antique cruet by washing it thoroughly with scalding water. Add the bird peppers and pour the sherry over them. Stopper the bottle and allow it to stand for several days. Pour a few drops in soups, stews, or whatever to enhance the dish's flavor. As you are only using the aromatic sherry, you have provided yourself with a never ending supply. When the sherry runs low, add more to the cruet, let stand a few days, and voilà . . . more sherry peppers.

PEPPER RUM

The principle is the same as for Sherry Peppers, above; however, the dark and fiery taste of pepper rum speaks more to the true flavor of the Caribbean. Use a medium rum such as Appelton Dark or Myer's Dark.

⅓ CUP MIXED BIRD PEPPERS AND   1¼ CUPS MEDIUM DARK RUM

   SCOTCH BONNET—TYPE CHILES

MAKES 1½ CUPS   Follow the instructions for preparing Sherry Peppers in the preceding recipe.

PRESERVED LIMES

These would seem to be the Caribbean version of Moroccan preserved lemons. They can be used for marinades or in stews. The limes should always be removed carefully, as any moisture that gets into the jar will spoil the remaining limes.

12 LIMES   2¼ CUPS EXTRA-VIRGIN OLIVE

12 WHOLE CLOVES   OIL, OR TO COVER

6 ALLSPICE BERRIES, 3 CRUSHED

1 SMALL SCOTCH BONNET—TYPE

   CHILE, STEM REMOVED AND

   SUN-DRIED FOR 2 OR 3 DAYS

12 LIMES   Wash and dry 12 firm limes and stick one clove into each lime. Place the allspice berries and the chile in a jar large enough to hold the limes. Place the limes in the jar and add the oil to cover the limes. Cork the jar and place it in a cool, dark place for 2 months. After 2 months, the limes are ready for use. The oil may also be used in salad dressings and marinades.

PINEAPPLE CHUTNEY

In the month of July, it is difficult to drive along the road that leads from Kingston to the north shore without seeing any number of small roadside stands set up selling pineapples. There are many varieties of pineapple, all known by name to Jamaicans. The most prized, however, is the sugar loaf, which has the shape of old-fashioned loaf sugar and is unbelievably sweet to northern taste buds. When combined with such typically Jamaican ingredients as dark brown sugar, cane vinegar, Scotch Bonnet pepper, and ginger, it produces a chutney that is the perfect foil for barbecues and grilled dishes.

3 CUPS FRESH CRUSHED
    PINEAPPLE
1 THUMB-SIZE PIECE OF FRESH
    GINGER, SCRAPED AND MINCED
1 SCOTCH BONNET—TYPE CHILE

1 MEDIUM-SIZE ONION, CHOPPED
1 CUP CANE VINEGAR
1 CUP DARK BROWN SUGAR

MAKES 2 CUPS   Chop the pineapple, ginger, chile, and onion in a food processor or blender. (You may have to add some of the vinegar to moisten the mixture if using a blender.) Place the mixture in a small nonreactive saucepan. Add the vinegar and sugar, stirring well to be sure that the ingredients are evenly distributed and there are no clumps of chile. Place the saucepan over medium heat and bring to a boil, stirring constantly to avoid sticking. Reduce the heat to low and continue to cook, stirring occasionally, until the chutney thickens, about 25 minutes. Pour the chutney into scalded glass jars. May be kept in the refrigerator for up to 3 weeks.

MANGO CHUTNEY

The Caribbean nation of Guyana is actually on the northern coast of South America. An extremely large number of Indians migrated to Guyana as indentured workers during the post-slavery period to toil on the remaining plantations. The result is that Mother India influences much Guyanese cooking. Curries abound, and they are more often than not accompanied by a dazzling array of condiments such as this mango chutney.

2 CUPS MANGO PULP

1 CLOVE GARLIC

1 SCOTCH BONNET—TYPE CHILE

1 THUMB-SIZE PIECE OF FRESH
    GINGER, SCRAPED

¼ TEASPOON SALT

½ CUP CANE VINEGAR

½ CUP DEMERARA SUGAR OR
    LIGHT BROWN SUGAR

MAKES 1½ CUPS   Place the mango pulp, garlic, chile, ginger, and salt into the bowl of a food processor or blender and mix to a smooth puree. Transfer the mixture to a small nonreactive saucepan, add the vinegar and sugar, and bring to a boil, stirring occasionally to mix all the ingredients well. Reduce the heat and continue to cook over a low flame until the mixture has thickened, about 25 minutes, stirring occasionally to make sure that the chutney does not stick. Remove the chutney from the heat. Allow it to cool and place in sterilized glass jars.

This recipe yields a small batch of chutney for immediate consumption, but it can be expanded. If processing large amounts, be sure to follow proper canning procedures to inhibit the growth of bacteria.

A small unprocessed batch will keep in the refrigerator for up to a month. If the recipe is doubled or quadrupled and prepared according to canning procedures, it will keep for up to six months without refrigeration.

GINGER-BANANA
CHUTNEY

Most people think of Trinidad, Guyana, and Martinique when they think of East Indian influences on Caribbean cooking. Jamaica, however, has had its share of that influence as well, as proved by this chutney that is prepared from bananas and ginger.

1 POUND ONIONS, CHOPPED

6 RIPE BANANAS, PUT THROUGH A
　FOOD MILL

¾ POUND PITTED DATES,
　CHOPPED

1 ½ CUPS CIDER VINEGAR

¼ POUND CRYSTALLIZED GINGER,
　MINCED

½ POUND RAISINS, CHOPPED

2 CUPS FRESH OR UNSWEETENED
　CANNED PINEAPPLE JUICE

1 TEASPOON SALT

2 TEASPOONS CURRY POWDER

MAKES ABOUT 3½ CUPS　Place the onions, bananas, dates, and vinegar in a nonreactive saucepan. Stir them to mix well and cook over low heat for 20 minutes. Add the remaining ingredients and stir to make sure they are well combined. Continue to cook until the chutney has a jamlike consistency. Remove from the heat and place in sterilized jars. This chutney can accompany cold meats, grilled meats and, of course, curries. It will keep for 3 weeks in the refrigerator.

PINEAPPLE JAM

Many travelers are surprised to find pineapples in such abundance at Caribbean roadside stands. They are frequently found in Caribbean fruit baskets, in desserts, drinks, and even on the breakfast table as pineapple jam.

ABOUT 2 CUPS FRESH PINEAPPLE CHUNKS

1 ½ CUPS SUGAR

DASH OF GRATED NUTMEG

DASH OF GROUND ALLSPICE

MAKES ABOUT 2 CUPS   Place the pineapple chunks in a food processor and chop them into a pulp. Put the pineapple pulp and sugar into a nonreactive saucepan, and bring the mixture to a boil over a medium flame, stirring well to be sure that the mixture does not stick to the pan bottom and that all of the sugar has melted. When the mixture has thickened into a jamlike consistency, about 30 minutes, remove from the heat and place in sterilized jars. It will keep for about 4 weeks in the refrigerator. The jam is great at breakfast time and is also a different accompaniment to grilled meats.

MAMBA

This peanut butter with a Caribbean accent is a hallmark of Haitian tables. I first discovered mamba, along with shaddock marmalade and cane syrup, among the condiments on the breakfast table at the Villa Créole in Pétionville, a Port-au-Prince suburb. I rediscovered mamba in the bustling open market where country women dispensed it from large aluminum pots and finally purchased some at the airport as I was preparing to leave. Mamba is prepared like peanut butter, but with a twist that comes from the addition of one or more of the fiery red peppers that are Haiti's answer to Jamaica's Scotch Bonnets. Looking very much like squashed Chinese lanterns, these peppers have a more orange hue than the Scotch Bonnet, but the same bite and, more important, the same taste. They are increasingly available in large cities where they can be found in Caribbean markets. In some areas in New York, they're simply known as Haitian pepper.

2 CUPS DARK ROASTED PEANUTS   SALT TO TASTE

3 TEASPOONS PEANUT OIL

1 OR MORE HAITIAN-TYPE CHILES,
   SEEDED

MAKES 1½ CUPS   Place the peanuts, peanut oil, and the chile in a food processor and grind to the desired crunchiness. Add salt to taste and stir to mix in the salt. You may add more or less chile as your taste buds dictate. You'll never think of a fluffernutter again.

GARLIC VINEGAR

One of the features of the Club Méditerranée on Paradise Island is a mealtime buffet that literally groans under a wide range of delicacies. The salad bar is particularly splendid with its tropical fruits. However, the items that most intrigued me were the various vinegars and oils that had been prepared by infusing local herbs, vegetables, and spices. Imagine my delight when, in reading accounts of Caribbean meals in the seventeenth century, I found that this tradition had a long history in the region. One of the favorite vinegars was garlic vinegar, used in marinades.

1 MEDIUM-SIZE HEAD OF GARLIC   2 CUPS CIDER VINEGAR

3 BIRD PEPPERS

2 TEASPOONS JAPANESE SOY
   SAUCE

MAKES 2 CUPS   Remove the skins from the garlic cloves and crush half of them with a mallet. Mix all of the ingredients together in a well-washed bottle with a stopper. Allow the vinegar to mature in the sun for 3 or more days. It can be used in salad dressings, marinades, and sauces.

THYME OIL

The principle here is the same as for the preparation of a flavored vinegar. The distinction is that the better the olive oil, the better the flavored oil.

8 BRANCHES FRESH THYME   2 CUPS EXTRA-VIRGIN OLIVE OIL

2 BIRD PEPPERS

MAKES 2 CUPS Place the ingredients, except 2 branches of thyme, in a small saucepan and heat them over a low flame for 10 minutes to allow the flavors to begin to infuse.

Allow the oil to cool and pour it into a bottle into which you have placed 2 branches of thyme for decoration. Stopper the bottle and place it in a dark place for 3 days. Use the oil for grilling, salad dressings, and in marinades.

ALL ISLANDS

CARIBBEAN PEPPER OIL

This oil has a fiery tang that makes it perfect for marinades and grilled meat. Those who like the spicy side of things might even wish to use it in an incendiary salad dressing. A liberal amount of chile is used along with the traditional seasoning herbs and spices of the region.

1 SHALLOT, MINCED

1 SCALLION, INCLUDING GREEN
   TOP, MINCED

1 CLOVE GARLIC, MINCED

3 CHIVES, MINCED

1 SPRIG FRESH THYME, MINCED

1 SPRIG PARSLEY, MINCED

1 SCOTCH BONNET—TYPE CHILE,
   SEEDED AND COARSELY
   CHOPPED

2 BIRD PEPPERS

1¾ CUPS EXTRA-VIRGIN OLIVE OIL

MAKES 2 CUPS Mix all of the ingredients together and pour them into a bottle. Stopper the bottle and allow it to stand in a dark place for a week. Use sparingly.

SEASONING

There are as many different recipes for seasoning in Barbados as there are cooks. The basics remain the same: thyme, garlic, parsley, onion, chile. I first came across seasoning on the rugged eastern side of the island in an area known to Bajans as Scotland. There a master cook nicknamed Scotty went to her icebox and removed a small jar. The mixture had the look of fresh moss from a northern forest and the aroma—the aroma was simply captivating. There was a hint of thyme with the pungency of garlic and enough of a bite to let you know that there was chile in there somewhere. To smell it was to love it, and it is indeed delicious when placed into scored cuts made in chicken or fish that is to be fried. Seasoning will keep for weeks in the refrigerator and is usually made in fairly large quantities. You may enlarge the recipe by doubling the quantities if you wish.

1 MEDIUM ONION

1 CLOVE GARLIC

3 CHIVES

2 SCALLIONS, INCLUDING GREEN
  TOPS

½ SCOTCH BONNET—TYPE CHILE

2 SPRIGS FRESH THYME

2 SPRIGS FLAT-LEAF ITALIAN
  PARSLEY

1 SPRIG FRESH MARJORAM

2 ALLSPICE BERRIES

½ TEASPOON SALT

MAKES ABOUT 1 CUP   Place all of the ingredients in a food processor and chop until the mixture is a thick paste. Put the mixture into containers that seal well.

JERKED SEASONING

Jerked pork (page 152) is a traditional Jamaican dish that has rapidly become a favorite with visitors from the States. The spicy jerk seasoning forms a wet marinade for the pork and gives the dish a piquant bite. Each Jamaican pork pit has its own ingredients. This is, perhaps, a milder version than most and can also be used on chicken.

½ CUP ALLSPICE BERRIES

1 1-INCH STICK CINNAMON

2 TEASPOONS GRATED NUTMEG

10 SCALLIONS, INCLUDING THE
  GREEN TOPS, MINCED

1 MEDIUM-SIZE ONION, MINCED

3 SCOTCH BONNET—TYPE CHILES,
  SEEDED AND MINCED

SALT AND FRESHLY GROUND
  BLACK PEPPER TO TASTE

2 TABLESPOONS DARK JAMAICAN
  RUM

MAKES 1 CUP　　Place the allspice berries on a baking sheet and bake them in a 350° oven for 5 minutes. Place the freshly roasted allspice berries, cinnamon, and nutmeg in a spice mill and grind them to a powder. Place the powder in a mortar and add the remaining ingredients. Pound into a thick paste.

SOFRITO

Puerto Rico's sofrito is a Hispanic answer to Barbados's Seasoning (see recipe above). A staple in all kitchens, it is added to soups, stews, and other dishes. There are numerous ways to prepare sofrito. This method prepares the vegetables, herbs, and spices first and then sautés them with pork products prior to use. Sofrito can be purchased ready-made at shops selling Hispanic products; however, it keeps well in the refrigerator and is easy to prepare.

2 GREEN BELL PEPPERS, SEEDED AND COARSELY CHOPPED

2 TOMATOES, PEELED, SEEDED, AND COARSELY CHOPPED

1 MEDIUM-SIZE ONION, CHOPPED

3 CLOVES GARLIC, CRUSHED

2 SPRIGS FRESH CORIANDER

1 SPRIG FLAT-LEAF ITALIAN PARSLEY

1 TABLESPOON LARD

1 TEASPOON CLEANED ACHIOTE

¼ POUND HAM, MINCED

¼ POUND SALT PORK, MINCED

MAKES 1½ CUPS   Place the bell peppers, tomatoes, onion, garlic, coriander, and parsley in a blender and mix until a smooth paste. (This can be kept in the refrigerator in a sterilized glass jar.)

Heat the lard in a skillet and add the achiote, which has been cleaned and picked over. Cook over medium heat for 10 minutes, until the oil has taken on a orangish hue. (This oil can be prepared in advance and kept in the refrigerator.)

When ready to prepare a dish calling for sofrito, sauté the vegetable and herb mixture in the oil, along with the ham and salt pork. Be sure that they sauté and do not fry. Chopped stuffed olives and a pinch of dried oregano may be added to the sofrito before using it in a variety of Puerto Rican recipes, such as Asopao de Pollo (page 168).

SEASONING

While seasoning in Barbados and the southern Caribbean is based on a thyme, parsley, garlic, and chile mixture, and Puerto Rico's Sofrito (preceding recipe) places the accent on bell peppers, tomatoes, garlic, and pork, the seasonings in the United States Virgin Islands are salt based and perfect for dry marinades. These essentially seasoned salts are extremely flavorful and can rapidly become the seasoning that you reach for first. (Those on low- or no-sodium diets may find that this is a good way to add extra tang to their own salt substitute.)

1 TEASPOON DRIED PARSLEY

1 TEASPOON DRIED THYME

1 TEASPOON DRIED CHIVES

¼ TEASPOON GARLIC POWDER

1 TEASPOON FRESHLY GROUND
    BLACK PEPPER

2 ALLSPICE BERRIES

1 TABLESPOON SEA SALT

MAKES 2 TABLESPOONS   Place the ingredients into a mortar or a spice grinder and grind them into a fine powder. The recipe is for a small amount, but the same proportions may be used to make a larger batch, which will keep indefinitely in a bottle or container with a top that does not corrode.

LIME PEPPER

For many, nothing is as much a part of Caribbean marinades as lime. The juice appears in numerous recipes, while the fruit figures in salad dressings, marinades, drinks, and desserts.

2 TEASPOONS DRIED LIME ZEST

1 TEASPOON DRIED LEMON ZEST

1 TEASPOON FRESHLY GROUND
   BLACK PEPPER

1 TEASPOON SEA SALT

MAKES 1½ TABLESPOONS   Place the ingredients in a spice grinder or mortar and pestle and grind until you have a well-mixed powder. Use to season everything from steaks to fish to salads.

NOTE ● *To prepare the dried lemon and lime zest, cut the zest from a lime and a lemon, dry it by placing it on a cookie sheet in a low (150°) oven for 24 hours. Then break it into small pieces and pulverize it in a spice grinder.*

ADOBO

This sauce is basic to many Puerto Rican recipes. It appears on virtually everything, either slathered on as a marinade or added as a seasoning. Try a bit when cooking meat.

5 CLOVES GARLIC, MINCED

1 TEASPOON DRIED OREGANO

2 TABLESPOONS OLIVE OIL

½ CUP WINE VINEGAR

MAKES ½ CUP   Mix the ingredients together in a small jar. You can use the adobo as a marinade for steak or for other meats. Simply slather it on and allow the meat to marinate for 24 hours or so in the refrigerator.

JAMAICA

RED DEVIL

PEPPER

SAUCE

Pepper sauces are one of the Caribbean region's inheritances from the pre-Columbian Native American cultures. They come in a variety of hues and in a variety of flavors. They have brilliant red coloring in Jamaica, perhaps indicative of the liberal addition of the incendiary Scotch Bonnet chiles that are typical of that country's cooking. This Jamaican version should be used sparingly because it is truly, truly hot.

6 SCOTCH BONNET—TYPE CHILES	1 TEASPOON KETCHUP
3 MEDIUM-SIZE ONIONS, DICED	1 TEASPOON PICKAPEPPA SAUCE
2 ALLSPICE BERRIES, CRUSHED	2 CUPS DISTILLED VINEGAR

MAKES 2 CUPS   Place the chiles, onions, and crushed allspice in the bowl of a food processor and mince until fine. In a small nonreactive saucepan, add the remaining ingredients to the chile mixture and bring to a boil, stirring occasionally. Allow to cool and place the pepper sauce in a bottle. It will keep for several months in the refrigerator. Use sparingly to accompany stews, grilled meats, and whatever you feel could use a bit of the devil.

CREOLE VINAIGRETTE

It is said that the classic vinaigrette dressing requires a miser for vinegar, a spendthrift for oil, and a gourmet for seasoning. The same holds true for this creole vinaigrette which makes use of some of the region's flavored oils and vinegars. You can add additional ingredients to this, such as roasted coconut, a spritz of dark rum, or a bit more chile. The recipe is a basic theme on which the variations are endless.

¼ CUP GARLIC VINEGAR (PAGE 116)

SALT AND FRESHLY GROUND BLACK PEPPER TO TASTE

PINCH OF SUGAR

½ TEASPOON DIJON-TYPE MUSTARD

½ CUP CARIBBEAN PEPPER OIL (PAGE 117)

MAKES 1¼ CUPS   Combine the vinegar, seasonings, sugar, and mustard in a small nonreactive bowl and whisk them well with a fork or wire whisk. Gradually drizzle in the pepper oil, continuing to whisk until the vinaigrette is well mixed.

VEGETABLES

AND

SALADS

●

"Going down to Linstead Market . . ." The Jamaican folk song tells of the joys of shopping in one of that country's open markets. It does not, however, go on to describe the delights of bargaining with one of Jamaica's own higglers.

Ample or wiry; dressed in peacock-hued calico dresses, with brimmed straw hats perched rakishly on their heads, they have the ability to charm the cash right out of your pocket. They hold forth seated behind their goods: escallion, Scotch Bonnet peppers, potatoes, tomatoes, onions. Alternately charmingly coy and annoyingly aggressive, they are at the same time a holdover from the past and a force in contemporary Jamaica's economy.

Unable to get to the market? Not to worry. The higglers also make house calls, and anyone who has lived in a Jamaican villa for long becomes used to hearing the higgler's cry: "Try these sugarloafs, they're so-o-o-o sweet, hyeah!"

JAMAICA

BOILED GREEN

BANANAS

In 1988, I had the dubious pleasure of spending the duration of Hurricane Gilbert in Jamaica. The devastation the hurricane caused this lovely island was immeasurable. However, as all clouds have their proverbial silver lining, so did Gilbert. My friend, Maria Williams, has banana trees on her property in Jamaica. When the hurricane blew many hands of green bananas down, we were provided with a traditional Jamaican breakfast treat, boiled green bananas. Definitely an acquired taste, these boiled bananas provide the starch in many Caribbean meals and are the traditional accompaniment for the French Antilles' Crasé de Morue (page 186).

8 MEDIUM-SIZE GREEN BANANAS,   WATER TO COVER
    PEELED (SEE GLOSSARY)   SALT TO TASTE

SERVES 6   In a heavy saucepan put the water and salt and bring to a boil. Place the bananas in the boiling water. Cook for about 15 minutes, remove, and serve hot.

MOFONGO

This Puerto Rican dish calls for plantains that are yellow and ripe. A traditional accompaniment to just about everything, it is particularly good with a soup or stew on a wet day. The shops across the street from the marketplace at Rio Piedras where much of San Juan's produce is bought and sold are noted as the best places in San Juan to eat mofongo. The dish, accompanied by a rum drink or a chilled beer, is virtually a meal in itself with its mixture of starchy plantain and the crispy chicharrones (fried pork rinds).

4 RIPE YELLOW PLANTAINS

VEGETABLE OIL FOR FRYING

½ POUND FRIED PORK RINDS (SEE
  NOTE)

1 TEASPOON SALT

4 CLOVES GARLIC

SERVES 2 TO 4   Peel the plantains and cut them into rondels. Heat the vegetable oil to 350° to 375° for frying in a heavy cast-iron pot or a deep fryer. Drop the plantain slices into the oil and fry them until they are well cooked but not crisp.

Meanwhile, place the pork rinds, salt, and garlic in a large mortar and pound them together. Add the plantain as it is cooked, continuing to pound them into a very thick paste. If you don't have a mortar and pestle, you may use a food processor: Pulse the ingredients until they reach the proper consistency. Form the paste into balls and warm them in a 300° oven for 5 minutes before serving.

The balls of mofongo are either served in a hearty chicken stock or mashed into small patties and served to accompany a variety of meat dishes.

N O T E • *Fried pork rinds are available packaged as snacks in supermarkets in urban areas. However, for a truly authentic mofongo, try to make your own Chicharrón (page 89). Or buy some freshly made chicharrones in a Latin American neighborhood.*

BANANES JAUNES AU GRATIN DES DEUX FROMAGES

The classic French béchamel sauce and the tropical banana come together in this dish. The slightly sweet taste of the banana makes it a perfect foil for the gratin prepared with grated Gruyère cheese. For a slightly more nouvelle cuisine touch, I have added the mildly tart taste of a crumbled goat cheese as well.

6 VERY RIPE BANANAS

¼ CUP FLOUR

¼ CUP (½ STICK) BUTTER

2 CUPS MILK

SALT AND FRESHLY GROUND
  BLACK PEPPER TO TASTE

DASH OF FRESHLY GRATED
  NUTMEG

¼ CUP GRATED GRUYÈRE CHEESE

¼ CUP CRUMBLED CHÈVRE

SERVES 4   Preheat the oven to 400°. Place the bananas in water to cover and cook them over a medium flame for 15 minutes, or until they are tender. Remove the bananas, peel them, cut them into pieces, and arrange them in a casserole dish.

Prepare a béchamel sauce by heating the flour in the butter in a sauce-pan over low heat. Slowly add the milk and the seasonings, stirring constantly to be sure that the ingredients are well mixed, until you have a thick sauce. Add the cheeses to the sauce, reserving half of each to garnish the top of the casserole. Pour the béchamel over the bananas. Sprinkle the remaining cheese over the top of the dish and bake for 20 minutes. Serve hot to accompany meat or fish dishes.

TOSTONES

These twice-fried plantain slices are a favorite accompaniment to many Puerto Rican dishes. Unlike their close cousins, Mofongo (page 130) and banane pesé, Tostones call for green plantains.

3 GREEN PLANTAINS

1 QUART COLD WATER

2 TEASPOONS ADOBO (PAGE 123,

   OR GOYA IS A RELIABLE

   BRAND.)

VEGETABLE OIL FOR FRYING

SERVES 2   Peel the green plantains, following the directions in the Glossary, and cut them into slices ½ inch thick. Place the slices in a bowl and cover them with the cold water into which you have mixed the adobo powder. Let them stand for about 10 minutes.

In a heavy cast-iron pot or a deep fryer, heat 1 inch of vegetable oil to 350° to 375° for frying. Remove the plantain slices from the water, reserving the water. Pat them dry with paper towels and drop them into the bubbling oil. Cook until they are well done, but not crisp, 5 to 7 minutes, turning if necessary. Remove the plantain slices from the oil and allow them to cool. When they have cooled enough to touch, press down on the slices, flattening them slightly, and replace them in the water for 5 minutes. Remove them from the water, and fry them again, this time cooking them until they are crispy. Remove, drain on paper towels, and serve hot.

BAKED SWEET POTATOES

Sweet potatoes are a traditional treat for New World Africans. In the seventeenth and eighteenth centuries these potatoes were cultivated in slave garden plots and baked in the ashes of cooking fires in the French Antilles.

Sweet potatoes are just fine plain with butter or margarine, or for those watching their weight or cholesterol, with a dollop of plain yogurt. This recipe uses rum, grated coconut, cinnamon, salt, and butter to enhance the flavor of the sweet potato.

6 MEDIUM-SIZE SWEET POTATOES

¼ CUP PEANUT OIL

3 TABLESPOONS DARK JAMAICAN
   RUM

2 TABLESPOONS BUTTER OR TO
   TASTE

2 TABLESPOONS FRESHLY GRATED
   COCONUT

SALT AND GROUND CINNAMON TO
   TASTE

SERVES 6   Wash the potatoes. Rub them with the oil and place them in an oven which has been preheated to 350°. Cook them for 1 hour, or until done.

Remove the sweet potatoes from the oven, cut a cross on the top of each one, and press the potato open with your fingers. With a spoon, scoop the potato meat into a medium-size bowl. Add the rum, butter, and coconut to the potato mixture; mix well and return the mixture to the potato shells. Sprinkle each shell with salt and cinnamon to taste. Place the filled sweet potato shells on a baking tin, return them to the oven, and continue to bake them for an additional 5 minutes, or until they are heated through. Serve at once.

RICE AND PEAS

If you call the dish rice and peas and make it with kidney beans, you're from Jamaica. There the dish is eaten so frequently, it's known as the Jamaican coat of arms. Call it peas and rice and you're from another part of the English-speaking Caribbean and may make this dish with pigeon peas or even yellow lentils. If you're Cuban, you'll know it as *moros y cristianos* and are used to the rice mixed with turtle beans or larger black beans. In Haiti, your *riz au pois* will have kidney beans in it, but in Martinique or Guadeloupe, it may include black-eyed peas, in which case they're *riz au z'yeux noirs*. If you still don't know what to call them in Puerto Rico, they're *arroz con gandules*.

½ POUND DRIED KIDNEY BEANS

2 TABLESPOONS PEANUT OIL

1 MEDIUM-SIZE ONION, MINCED

1 SCOTCH BONNET—TYPE CHILE,

   SEEDED AND MINCED

1 ½ CUPS BOTTLED OR HOMEMADE

   UNSWEETENED COCONUT MILK

1 SPRIG FRESH THYME

2 CHIVES, MINCED

SALT AND FRESHLY GROUND

   BLACK PEPPER TO TASTE

2 CUPS WHITE UNCOOKED RICE

SERVES 6   Prepare the dried kidney beans according to package directions and cook until almost tender. Drain the beans and reserve the cooking liquid. Return the beans to their cooking pot.

Heat the oil in a heavy skillet and brown the onion. Add the onion and the remaining ingredients to the bean pot along with 2½ cups of the reserved bean cooking liquid. (If there is not enough, add cold water to supplement.) Cover the pot and cook over low heat for 25 minutes, or until all the water has been absorbed and the rice is tender.

CORNMEAL COOCOO

Coocoo is one of the dishes that is emblematic of Africa's contribution to Caribbean cooking. A close New World relative of West Africa's mashes, which form the basis of many of that continent's stews and sauces, coocoo is traditionally eaten with fried or steamed fish. A slice of it is a necessary side dish in local restaurants. Coocoo becomes *funghi* in the U.S. Virgin Islands and *foofoo* on other islands. The trick in making the coocoo like its Italian cousin, polenta, is to keep stirring. Bajans use a coocoo stick or a paddle that is designed to "turn" the coocoo more easily than a spoon. You can try with a spoon, but I've had better luck with a paint stirrer.

¼ POUND FRESH OKRA, TOPPED, TAILED, AND CUT INTO ¼-INCH SLICES

3½ CUPS WATER

2 CUPS YELLOW CORNMEAL

1 TEASPOON SALT

2 TABLESPOONS SUGAR

2 TABLESPOONS UNSALTED BUTTER

SERVES 6   Put the okra in a heavy saucepan with ¾ cup of the water and boil until tender. Remove from the heat and reserve the okra and the liquid.

Meanwhile, in a bowl, soak the cornmeal in 1½ cups of the water to which the salt and sugar have been added. Place the remaining 1¼ cups of water in a medium-size saucepan and bring it to a boil. When the water is boiling, stir in the cornmeal with a coocoo stick or wooden spoon and add the butter. Fold in the reserved okra and liquid.

Place 3 inches of water in the bottom of a pot large enough to hold the pot containing the okra and cornmeal mixture. Place the pot containing the okra and cornmeal mixture inside the larger pot, cover it, and allow the mixture to steam for 15 minutes. Stir every 5 minutes and make sure that the water in the larger pot remains at a slow boil; add more hot water if necessary.

When the cornmeal coocoo is done, remove it from the heat, cool it for 5 minutes, and place half of the mixture in a greased round bowl. Roll the bowl around to form a ball of coocoo. Continue in the same manner to form a second ball from the remaining coocoo. Coocoo should be served sliced and hot. It may be topped with a pat of butter.

STUFFED BREADFRUIT

Breadfruit, which was brought to the Caribbean by Captain Bligh, was first used as food for the slaves. However, after slavery's end, breadfruit was found to be a tasty vegetable and has appeared in many guises on many tables. This cannonball-shaped vegetable is served as French fries, as coocoo, roasted, and baked. Stuffed breadfruit is one of the more elegant ways it appears. If you add cooked ground beef or leftover chicken to this dish, it can become a main course.

1 MEDIUM-SIZE BREADFRUIT

¼ CUP HEAVY CREAM

1 TABLESPOON SLIGHTLY SALTED
  BUTTER

1 MEDIUM-SIZE ONION, MINCED

1 MEDIUM-SIZE TOMATO, PEELED,
  SEEDED, AND COARSELY
  CHOPPED

DASH OF FRESHLY GROUND
  ALLSPICE

SALT AND FRESHLY GROUND
  BLACK PEPPER TO TASTE

SERVES 6 TO 8   Roast the breadfruit. Ideally this is done over charcoal, but it can also be accomplished by placing the entire breadfruit on the gas burner and allowing it to cook, turning it as it begins to char. This will take about 1 hour.

When the breadfruit is roasted, remove it from the burner, cut a circle at the stem end, and scoop out the heart and discard it. Scoop out the breadfruit flesh, leaving a ¾-inch shell. Mix the breadfruit flesh with the cream and butter, then add the onion, tomato, and seasonings. Pack the breadfruit mixture back into the shell, wrap the breadfruit with foil, and place it in a 300° oven for 10 minutes to warm it thoroughly before serving. Unwrap the breadfruit and serve it whole on a platter; each diner serves him/herself from the shell.

PAK CHOI AND TOMATOES

What is called bok choy or Chinese cabbage in the Asian markets in the United States is known as pak choi or pe-tsai in much of the Caribbean. This dish is a gift to the region from the Chinese settlers who made their home in the islands in the late nineteenth and early twentieth centuries.

2 POUNDS BOK CHOY

SALT

1 CUP WATER

1 SMALL ONION, CHOPPED

2 MEDIUM-SIZE TOMATOES,
   PEELED, SEEDED, AND
   COARSELY CHOPPED

½ SCOTCH BONNET—TYPE CHILE
   OR TO TASTE, MINCED

SALT AND FRESHLY GROUND
   BLACK PEPPER TO TASTE

SERVES 6   Wash the bok choy, and cut it into small pieces. In a saucepan, add salt to the water and bring to a boil. Cook the bok choy in the boiling water for 10 minutes. Drain, and place the bok choy in a skillet with the onion, tomatoes, chile, and seasoning. Cook over low heat for 15 minutes. Serve hot.

YUCA FRITA

In the Caribbean, the duo of "meat and potatoes" still holds true. However, in the Caribbean region, it is often changed to "meat and starch." Yuca is one of the preferred starches, and it appears in many guises, fried being a favorite. Many Caribbean cooks keep a stock of boiled yuca in the refrigerator ready for preparation.

2 POUNDS YUCA

VEGETABLE OIL FOR FRYING

½ CUP VIRGIN OLIVE OIL

1 TABLESPOON MINCED PARSLEY,

   PLUS SPRIGS FOR GARNISH

2 GARLIC CLOVES, MINCED

SALT AND FRESHLY GROUND

   BLACK PEPPER TO TASTE

SERVES 6 TO 8   Wash the yuca, peel it, and cut it into 2-inch by 1-inch pieces. Boil it in salted water for 1 hour or until fork tender. Drain it and remove any fibrous pieces.

Heat 2 inches of oil for frying to 350° to 375° in a heavy cast-iron pot or a deep fryer. Place the yuca pieces into the bubbling oil a few at a time and fry until golden brown, turning once. Remove the pieces as done and drain them on paper towels.

Mix the remaining ingredients together and pour over the yuca frita. Garnish with parsley sprigs and serve warm.

OKRA CREOLE

In this dish, Africa's okra meets up with the corn, onion, green pepper, and tomato mixture that is typical of much of Caribbean cooking. Traditionally, this dish calls for bacon drippings, which add a wonderful taste. However, the cholesterol- or diet-conscious may choose to substitute an unsaturated oil, such as peanut oil.

1 LARGE ONION, SLICED

1 SMALL GREEN BELL PEPPER, CHOPPED

3 TABLESPOONS BACON DRIPPINGS OR PEANUT OIL

20 OKRA PODS, TOPPED, TAILED, AND SLICED

2 MEDIUM-SIZE TOMATOES, PEELED, SEEDED, AND COARSELY CHOPPED

1 CUP FRESH CORN KERNELS

SALT AND FRESHLY GROUND BLACK PEPPER TO TASTE

SERVES 8   In a heavy skillet, brown the onion and pepper in the bacon drippings. Then add the okra and cook them over medium heat for 5 minutes. Add the tomatoes and corn, lower the heat, and continue to cook for 15 minutes, or until the okra is fork tender. Season with salt and freshly ground black pepper and serve hot.

BROILED TOMATOES
ATLANTIS

The Atlantis Hotel on Barbados's wild Atlantic coast hosts a Sunday brunch that is a treat for food lovers. The hotel's owners carefully prepare a wide assortment of traditional and modern Bajan dishes and set them out in a luncheon buffet that is a culinary tour of the island. It was here that I first sampled broiled tomatoes. The dish is so simple, yet when prepared with fresh tangy tomatoes, it goes with almost any foods you can think of.

6 MEDIUM-SIZE TOMATOES, CORED

2 TABLESPOONS BUTTER

SALT AND FRESHLY GROUND

BLACK PEPPER TO TASTE

SERVES 6   Place the tomatoes in a broiler-proof dish. Dot the tops of the tomatoes with butter; season with salt and freshly ground black pepper. Place the tomatoes in the broiler and cook for 10 minutes, or until they are slightly browned on the tops. Serve hot with grilled meats.

MIGNAN DE
FRUIT À
PAIN

Mignan de fruit à pain, a pureed breadfruit dish, is traditional in the French-speaking Caribbean. There are numerous variations, some more appropriate as a main course, others more suited as a vegetable accompaniment. In this version, the bacon is simply used to season the breadfruit while it is cooking. In other versions, pig tails and other meats are used, then removed and served separately along with a peppery sauce chien.

½ POUND STREAKY BACON, CUT
   INTO ½-INCH CUBES

1 BOUQUET GARNI: 3 SPRIGS
   PARSLEY, 2 SPRIGS FRESH
   THYME, ½ BAY LEAF, 3
   PEPPERCORNS, 3 ALLSPICE
   BERRIES

1 SMALL SCOTCH BONNET—TYPE
   CHILE, PRICKED WITH A FORK

1 POUND FRESH BREADFRUIT

SERVES 6   Place the bacon in a large saucepan, add the bouquet garni and chile, and sear. Lower the heat to medium and continue to cook.

Meanwhile, peel the breadfruit, remove the core, and cut into large dice. Place the chopped breadfruit in the saucepan with the bacon and cook for 40 minutes. When the breadfruit is cooked, remove the bouquet garni and the chile, and whip the breadfruit and the bacon with a wooden spoon or a *baton lélé* (see Glossary) until the mixture is creamy. Serve hot.

MAMA'S PUMPKIN PUREE

Those who delight in traditional Caribbean food should consider taking a trip to Grenada for no other reason than to dine at Mama's, a small local restaurant outside of the capital. To say that the decor is unprepossessing is true understatement. There is no menu at Mama's. You simply sit down. No sooner than you've had a Rum Punch, lightly dusted with nutmeg in the Grenadian manner, than a parade of dishes begins; after the first ten you lose count. The waitress, one of Mama's family, will explain them to you. There's fish, beef, chicken, pork, and other familiar viands. Then come armadillo, iguana, and perhaps even monkey. Vegetables are stewed, steamed, fried, and pureed. The array is staggering and the dishes are all delicious. And so what if you turn your nose up at the monkey . . . there are so many other dishes, you won't go hungry and no one will know.

2 POUNDS CALABAZA

2 TABLESPOONS VEGETABLE OIL

3 CHIVES, MINCED

3 CLOVES GARLIC, MINCED

2 SPRIGS FRESH THYME OR ½
   TEASPOON DRIED

2 SPRIGS PARSLEY, MINCED

1 SMALL SCOTCH BONNET—TYPE
   CHILE, SEEDED AND CUT INTO
   PIECES

SALT AND FRESHLY GROUND
   BLACK PEPPER TO TASTE

SERVES 6   Peel the calabaza, cut into pieces, and place in a saucepan. Cover it with salted water and bring to a boil over medium heat. Reduce the heat and cook until the calabaza is fork tender.

Heat the oil in a heavy frying pan. Add the chives, garlic, thyme, parsley, and chile, and cook until the garlic is browned. When the calabaza is cooked, put it through a food mill. Add the pureed calabaza to the oil and seasoning mixture in the frying pan and cook for 2 to 3 minutes, adding salt and freshly ground black pepper. Serve hot.

PUMPKIN SALAD

The West Indian cooking pumpkin or calabaza has a lovely delicate taste, more flavorful than many squashes and yet milder than its North American cousin. It appears in stews, in nouvelle cuisine purees, and in hearty dishes like Mama's Pumpkin Puree (see preceding recipe). Here it turns up tossed in a vinaigrette dressing as salad.

1 SMALL HEAD OF ROMAINE
   LETTUCE, LEAVES WASHED AND
   SEPARATED

1½ POUNDS CALABAZA, BOILED,
   PEELED, AND CUT INTO 1-INCH
   PIECES

1 MEDIUM-SIZE RED BELL
   PEPPER, DICED

1 MEDIUM-SIZE GREEN BELL
   PEPPER, DICED

2 TABLESPOONS GARLIC VINEGAR
   (PAGE 116)

5 TABLESPOONS LIGHT OLIVE OIL

½ TEASPOON BROWN SUGAR

1 TEASPOON MINCED FRESH
   CHIVES

SERVES 4 TO 6 Arrange the romaine lettuce leaves on a medium-size platter. Mix the calabaza and bell peppers together. Prepare a vinaigrette from the remaining ingredients and pour it over the calabaza and bell pepper mixture. Mix well and place on top of the lettuce leaves. Place in the refrigerator for 30 minutes and serve chilled.

AVOCADO AND
GRAPEFRUIT
SALAD

Avocados and grapefruit are both native to the region and when combined make an excellent salad. Try adding a few cooked shrimp to this to make a perfect appetizer or a light luncheon dish.

2 RIPE AVOCADOS

2 MEDIUM-SIZE PINK GRAPEFRUIT

1 TABLESPOON FRESHLY
    SQUEEZED GRAPEFRUIT JUICE

1 TABLESPOON CANE VINEGAR

¼ CUP LIGHT OLIVE OIL

¼ TEASPOON FRESHLY GROUND
    ALLSPICE

PARSLEY SPRIGS AND CANDIED
    GRAPEFRUIT RIND FOR GARNISH

SERVES 4   Remove the pits from the avocados, peel them, and slice them lengthwise. Segment the grapefruit, making sure that all of the membrane is removed from the fruit. Reserve 1 tablespoon of the juice. Prepare a vinaigrette from the remaining ingredients, including the grapefruit juice.

Arrange the avocado and grapefruit on 4 salad plates in alternating bands. Drizzle the vinaigrette over them. Garnish with a sprig of parsley and a piece of candied grapefruit rind.

GREEK SALAD NORMA

Norma Shirley, a transplanted food stylist from New York, presides over one of new Kingston's choicest restaurants. The salads are always delicious in a region where salads are not usually served. Norma's Greek salad, with ruby circles of Otaheite apple, is a delight anywhere. This isn't the original recipe; it's a variation that can be made in northern kitchens where the Otaheite apple is only a part of vacation dreams.

1 HEAD OF ROMAINE LETTUCE	9 TABLESPOONS OLIVE OIL
1 SMALL MILD RED ONION, SLICED	¼ CUP CANE VINEGAR
1 MEDIUM-SIZE TOMATO, COARSELY CHOPPED	DASH OF DIJON-TYPE MUSTARD
	PINCH OF SUGAR
1 SMALL RED DELICIOUS APPLE, COARSELY CHOPPED	SALT AND FRESHLY GROUND BLACK PEPPER TO TASTE
½ SMALL CUCUMBER, COARSELY CHOPPED	¼ POUND GREEK FETA CHEESE

SERVES 6   Wash the lettuce and tear it into bite-size bits. Place the lettuce, onion, tomato, apple, and cucumber into a large salad bowl.

Prepare a vinaigrette from the oil, vinegar, mustard, sugar, and seasonings. Crumble the feta cheese over the top of the salad bowl, pour on the dressing, and serve.

ÑAME À LA VINAIGRETTE

Yams, that is *true* yams, turn up everywhere in Caribbean cooking. This salad, which goes well with roast pork, is simply the traditional boiled yam served with a vinaigrette prepared from local spices and herbs.

2 POUNDS YAMS, PEELED AND BOILED

1 MEDIUM-SIZE ONION, THINLY SLICED

1 SMALL GREEN BELL PEPPER, THINLY SLICED CROSSWISE

9 TABLESPOONS OLIVE OIL

½ TEASPOON ADOBO (PAGE 123 OR GOYA BRAND)

¼ TEASPOON GROUND RED CHILE

¼ CUP GARLIC VINEGAR (PAGE 116)

1 BAY LEAF

SERVES 6   Cut the yam into 1-inch pieces. Place it in a bowl with the onion and bell pepper. Prepare a vinaigrette from the remaining ingredients and pour it over the contents of the bowl. Allow to sit for 30 minutes so that the yam can absorb the vinaigrette. Serve.

CHRISTOPHINE VINAIGRETTE

Christophine is the name chayote goes by in the French-speaking Caribbean. These puckered-up, lime-green vegetables have an incredibly mild meat, which takes on the flavor of any vinaigrette. This makes them perfect for a salad using a traditional creole vinaigrette which is spicy with chives, hot chile, and garlic.

2 MEDIUM-SIZE CHAYOTES

2 TABLESPOONS GARLIC VINEGAR
   (PAGE 116)

¼ CUP OLIVE OIL

¼ TEASPOON SCOTCH BONNET—
   TYPE CHILE

½ TEASPOON CHOPPED FRESH
   CHIVES

1 HEAD BIBB OR BOSTON
   LETTUCE, SEPARATED INTO
   LEAVES

RED BELL PEPPER FOR GARNISH

SERVES 4   Peel the chayotes and grate them into a bowl. Prepare
a vinaigrette from the remaining ingredients except the lettuce and pepper
and pour it over the grated chayotes. Mix well and allow to sit for 15
minutes.

   Serve on a bed of lettuce garnished with curlicues of red bell pepper.

MARTINIQUE

SALADE DE CHOU
PALMISTE

For anyone who loves the briny crunch of hearts of palm, the Caribbean
islands seem to be heaven. Here hearts of palm quite literally grow in
trees; they form the inner heart of the palm tree. While folks in the
Caribbean prepare the fresh hearts of palm, we in the northern climes are
reduced to purchasing them in cans. If you get your hands on fresh hearts
of palm, peel them down to the tenderest interior segments and use them
in the delicate salad.

1 CAN OF HEARTS OF PALM

JUICE OF 1 LIME

SALT AND FRESHLY GROUND
   BLACK PEPPER TO TASTE

SERVES 2   Drain the hearts of palm and slice them lengthwise
into julienne strips. Drizzle lime juice over them and season to taste.

MAIN

DISHES

Hearty dishes are the hallmark of Caribbean cooking. While restaurants try to emulate them, none have the home-cooked flavor of a family meal. For me, the best compromise is a roadside stand.

The drive along the north coast of the Dominican Republic from Puerto Plata to Playa Grande was not long and took me through rolling cane fields and small towns where folks had gathered for market day. As we drove by pens of squealing pigs, my driver promised me that on the way back we'd be able to find some *chicharrón de cerdo,* roasted pork with cracklings. My mouth immediately started to water in anticipation. The beauty of the pristine rain-swept beach at Playa Grande and a superb (not too creamy) piña colada served in the pineapple shell complete with pineapple chunks went a long way to diverting my attention. But no sooner were we back in the car and on the road than my taste buds started warming up for a treat. Finally, we arrived at a tiny shack by the side of the road. They had just finished giving the pig its final turn. It was sold by the pound complete with boiled yuca, corn on the cob, and lemon to squeeze over the pork, and served up on torn-up brown paper bags. The pork was sweet and not too fatty, the crackling better than caviar, and the yuca was the perfect accompaniment—complementing the sweetness of the pork with its bland, starchy texture. No restaurant food could compare.

CHICHARRÓN DE CERDO

In the Dominican Republic, chicharrón is prepared from large cuts of pork. At home, though, it is possible to get the same succulent taste and the same crackling skin.

1 6- TO 7-POUND FRESH HAM

¼ CUP VEGETABLE OIL

1 TABLESPOON DRIED ROSEMARY

1 TABLESPOON SALT

1 TEASPOON FRESHLY GROUND
BLACK PEPPER

SERVES 8 TO 10   Preheat the oven to 450°. Place the fresh ham in a roasting pan, skin side up, and score the skin into 1-inch squares. Rub the ham with the oil, rosemary, salt, and pepper and place it in the oven. Bake for 15 minutes; then lower the heat to 350°. Continue to roast for 30 minutes per pound. When done, serve the pork with a bit of the crackling skin on each plate.

JERKED PORK

It is said that the Maroons, or escaped renegade slaves who lived up in the Cockpit country of the Blue Mountains, developed this classic Jamaican dish. Lady Nugent, the wife of one of the island's British governors, tasted jerked boar and was so taken with it that she asked for the recipe and reproduced it in her diary. Today, tasting can be done at any of the numerous pork pits that dot the Montego Bay to Ocho Rios highway. Traditionally, the best place for jerked pork in Jamaica is at Boston Bay near Port Antonio, but wherever you have it, the taste of the meat slow cooked over a fire of green allspice branches gives the dish an unforgettable flavor. Since allspice logs are not found in the States, this recipe calls for pork loin and uses an oven, but you can also use an outdoor grill.

¼ CUP ALLSPICE BERRIES

1 ½-INCH PIECE OF CINNAMON
STICK

1 TEASPOON GRATED NUTMEG

6 SCALLIONS, INCLUDING GREEN
TOPS, SLICED

1 SCOTCH BONNET—TYPE CHILE
OR TO TASTE

SALT AND FRESHLY GROUND
BLACK PEPPER

1 TABLESPOON DARK JAMAICA
RUM

1 4-POUND BONED PORK LOIN

SERVES 8   Roast the allspice berries in a 350° oven for 10 minutes. Pulverize them in a spice mill with the cinnamon and nutmeg. Place the spice mixture in a mortar with the scallions, chile, and salt and pepper and grind into a paste. Add the rum. Rub the mixture all over the pork loin. Cover and allow to marinate for at least 1 hour at room temperature.

Preheat the oven to 400°. Remove the meat from the marinade, place in a roasting pan, and roast in the oven for 30 minutes. Reduce the heat to 350° and continue to cook, basting with pan juices, for about 1½ hours. Transfer to a warm platter and serve hot. You can serve the jerked pork with peas and rice and one of the chutneys found in the chapter on Sauces, Condiments, and Seasonings.

COOK-UP RICE

When I told my friend June Bobb that I was going to be writing a Caribbean cookbook, I asked her for her favorite dish. She said that she was fond of Cook-Up Rice. You will not find it in restaurants, as it is truly home cooking. It's simple to make and utterly delicious.

2 TABLESPOONS VEGETABLE OIL

1 TEASPOON BROWN SUGAR

1 MEDIUM-SIZE ONION, DICED

2 TOMATOES, PEELED, SEEDED,
   AND COARSELY CHOPPED

2 SCALLIONS, INCLUDING THE
   GREEN TOPS, SLICED

1 BRANCH FRESH THYME OR ¼
   TEASPOON DRIED

¼ POUND SALT PORK, DICED

4½ CUPS WATER

2 CUPS UNCOOKED WHITE RICE

½ TEASPOON SALT

½ POUND COOKED STEAK OR
   ROAST BEEF, DICED

½ TEASPOON ANGOSTURA BITTERS

SERVES 4   Heat the oil in a heavy saucepan. Add the sugar and fry it until it bubbles. Add the onion, tomatoes, scallions, and thyme and fry until the onions are golden brown. Add the salt pork, water, rice, and salt and bring to a boil over medium heat. Cook until the rice is nearly done, then add the diced cooked meat. Just prior to serving, add the angostura bitters, stir, and serve.

COLOMBO DE PORC

Much to the surprise of many visitors, Martinique has a sizable Indian population. From their subcontinent home, they have brought with them their customs, their religion, and their foods. To the traditional taste of southern India and Sri Lanka's curries, the transplanted West Indians would add allspice berries. Meats that traditionally would be anathema for devout Hindus in India are the basis for some of the most prized curries in the New World. In the French-speaking Caribbean, this dish takes its name from that of the capital of Sri Lanka, Colombo.

3 TABLESPOONS BUTTER

2 TABLESPOONS OLIVE OIL

2 POUNDS PORK LOIN, CUT INTO
   BITE-SIZE PIECES

1 MEDIUM-SIZE ONION, COARSELY
   CHOPPED

2 SCALLIONS, INCLUDING GREEN
   TOPS, MINCED

1 SHALLOT, MINCED

2 TABLESPOONS CURRY POWDER

4 ALLSPICE BERRIES

1 CLOVE GARLIC, MINCED

2 BRANCHES FRESH THYME OR ½
   TEASPOON DRIED

3 SPRIGS FRESH PARSLEY,
   MINCED

3 TABLESPOONS WATER

1 TABLESPOON WHITE WINE
   VINEGAR

SALT AND FRESHLY GROUND
   BLACK PEPPER TO TASTE

1 SCOTCH BONNET—TYPE CHILE,
   PRICKED WITH A FORK

1 CHAYOTE, PEELED, CUT INTO 1-
   INCH PIECES

1 SMALL EGGPLANT, PEELED AND
   CUT INTO 1-INCH PIECES

2 MEDIUM-SIZE TOMATOES,
   PEELED, SEEDED, AND
   COARSELY CHOPPED

SERVES 4 TO 6   Heat the butter and oil in a heavy frying pan over medium heat. Add the pork, onion, scallions, and shallot, and cook, stirring occasionally, until the pork pieces are browned on all sides.

   Place the curry powder into a spice mill with the allspice grains and grind until they are well mixed. Add the curry mixture to the frying pan along with the garlic, thyme, and parsley. Cover with the water and vinegar, lower the heat, and cook for 30 minutes. Season with the salt and pepper and add the chile, chayote, eggplant, and tomatoes. Continue to cook, uncovered, stirring occasionally, until the curry has a thick sauce (you may need to add a bit more water). Serve the colombo de porc hot with white rice.

GRIOTS DE PORC

These pork bits, which are sometimes called *grillots,* are a typical Haitian treat traditionally served in Voodoo temples, or *hommfors,* during ceremonies for Azaka, the loa (deity) of the hunt and the out-of-doors. In this case, the dish is prepared from the pig that has been sacrificed to the loa. However, the dish is also found on hotel menus and in private homes, where the source of the meat is more apt to be the local butcher shop.

1 POUND PORK LOIN, CUT INTO 1-INCH PIECES

1 CUP FRESHLY SQUEEZED LIME JUICE

½ CUP FRESHLY SQUEEZED ORANGE JUICE

5 CHIVES, MINCED

1 SCOTCH BONNET—TYPE CHILE, MINCED

2 CLOVES GARLIC, MINCED

1 LARGE ONION, MINCED

SALT AND FRESHLY GROUND BLACK PEPPER TO TASTE

SERVES 4   Wash the pork pieces with half of the lime juice. Prepare a marinade from the remaining ingredients and place the pork pieces in the marinade for at least 1 hour. Then transfer the pork pieces and marinade to a heavy cast-iron casserole; cover with cold water. Bring the casserole to a boil over medium heat, then lower the heat and continue to cook, uncovered, until the liquid evaporates and nothing remains but a thick brown sauce and the cooked pork bits. Serve hot with white rice.

CHOP SUEY

My Guyanese friend will occasionally prepare a chop suey for family and friends. The dish is not difficult to prepare, just time consuming, because all of the vegetables must be julienned. This, though, can be done in preparation hours before the final steps.

4 MEDIUM-SIZE CHAYOTES,
   PEELED AND JULIENNED

1 POUND BOK CHOY, JULIENNED

6 CARROTS, JULIENNED

3 LARGE ONIONS, THINLY SLICED

15 SCALLIONS, INCLUDING GREEN
   TOPS, COARSELY CHOPPED

3 POUNDS SKINLESS, BONELESS
   CHICKEN BREAST, DICED

2 POUNDS LEAN PORK, DICED

2 CLOVES GARLIC, MINCED

1 TABLESPOON SUGAR

2 TEASPOONS SALT

1 TABLESPOON CORNSTARCH

1 TEASPOON 5-SPICE POWDER

FRESHLY GROUND BLACK PEPPER
   TO TASTE

2 TABLESPOONS COLD WATER

2 TABLESPOONS SOY SAUCE

1 ¼ CUPS VEGETABLE OIL

1 POUND MUNG BEAN SPROUTS

2 POUNDS SMALL SHRIMP,
   PEELED AND CLEANED

SERVES 12   Place the julienned chayotes, bok choy, carrots, onions, and scallions in a bowl of iced water in the refrigerator. Place the diced chicken and pork in a bowl with the garlic, the sugar, 1 teaspoon of the salt, the cornstarch, 5-spice powder, pepper, cold water, and soy sauce and mix them together thoroughly until the meat is coated.

Place ¼ cup of the oil in a wok and heat it over a high flame until bubbling. Drain the vegetables and add them and the remaining teaspoon of salt. Stir-fry the vegetables rapidly until they are cooked, but not limp. Add the bean sprouts and continue to cook for a minute. Remove the vegetables to a bowl.

Heat the remaining 1 cup of oil in the wok, and stir-fry the chicken, pork, and shrimp for about 5 minutes, stirring frequently to make sure that the meat and shrimp are almost cooked. Add the vegetables on top of the meat and continue to cook until the meat is fully done. Serve hot with white rice.

NOTE ● *5-spice powder is available from Asian food stores. If unavailable, allspice can be substituted.*

GARLIC PORK

You don't have to ask your friends if they've had this traditional holiday dish on Christmas morning. If they have, the half pound of garlic included in the ingredients ensures that you will know when they drop in to bring you your Christmas gifts. Just in case you miss the aroma of garlic pork on Christmas morning, what's left is eaten on New Year's Day.

3 TO 4 POUNDS PORK LOIN, CUT
    INTO 1-INCH PIECES
3 CUPS WHITE VINEGAR
½ POUND GARLIC, SEPARATED
    INTO CLOVES AND PEELED
4 STALKS FRESH THYME OR
    1 TEASPOON DRIED

6 TO 8 WIRI WIRI—TYPE CHILES OR
    2 SCOTCH BONNET—TYPE
    CHILES
2 CUPS COLD WATER
2 TEASPOONS SALT
6 CLOVES
1 TABLESPOON VEGETABLE OIL

SERVES 6 TO 8   In a large bowl, wash the pork pieces with 1 cup of the vinegar. Lift them from the bowl with 2 large forks; do not use your hands. Place the pork in a large jar or bottle.

Place the peeled garlic, thyme, and chiles in a mortar and pound to a paste. Then add the cold water and the remaining 2 cups of vinegar to the garlic mixture. Add the salt and cloves and pour the garlic and vinegar mixture over the pork, making sure that the pork is completely covered. Tightly cover the jar and allow the pork to marinate in a cool place for 3 to 4 days or longer.

To cook, place the pork in a heavy skillet and cook until the liquid evaporates. Then add the vegetable oil and fry the pork until it is brown. Serve hot over white rice.

LOCRIO OF SALT PORK
AND LONGANIZA

A *locrio* is a Dominican stew that seems to be a close cousin of Puerto Rico's *asopaos*. There are a seemingly endless number of them, but some of the most common are made with salt pork, salt cod, or fresh pork. Whether in the private homes in the capital of Santo Domingo or out in the country where the weather can be surprisingly bracing in the hills, this stick-to-the-ribs dish is a welcome lunch or dinner. A traditional accompaniment would be a frosty beer or a glass of one of the Dominican Republic's three B's: Brugal, Barcelo, and Bermudez rum. The rums are almost as warming as the stew.

1 POUND SALT PORK	1 1-POUND PIECE OF CALABAZA,
1 LONGANIZA (DOMINICAN	PEELED AND DICED
SAUSAGE) OR CHORIZO	2 LARGE ONIONS, DICED
½ CUP OLIVE OIL	1 GREEN BELL PEPPER, DICED
3 MEDIUM-SIZE TOMATOES,	1 GALLON WATER
PEELED, SEEDED, AND	3 GARLIC CLOVES, MINCED
COARSELY CHOPPED	2 SPRIGS PARSLEY
¼ CUP TOMATO PASTE, DISSOLVED	1 SCOTCH BONNET—TYPE CHILE,
IN 1 CUP OF WATER	PRICKED WITH A FORK
1 LEEK, INCLUDING THE GREEN	2 CUPS UNCOOKED WHITE RICE
TOP, CLEANED AND CUT INTO	
PIECES	

SERVES 6 TO 8   Dice the pork and the Longaniza; wash and pat them dry with paper towels. Heat half of the oil in a heavy, medium-size saucepan. When the oil is hot, add the tomatoes, salt pork, and sausage and fry for about 4 minutes. Add the tomato paste, half of the leek, the calabaza, onions, and green pepper. Cover, lower the flame, and cook until the meat is tender.

Remove the ingredients from the heat and transfer them to a large stockpot in which the stew will be cooked. Add the water, remaining leek, and the garlic, parsley, and pricked chile. Cover and bring to a boil. When the locrio is boiling, add the rice and cook over a high flame for 10 minutes or until the rice is almost dry. Then add the remaining oil, cover, lower the heat, and cook for an additional 20 minutes. Serve hot, accompanied by a green salad.

PEPPERPOT

Pepperpot is one of the few signature Caribbean dishes that hark back to Arawak days. Cassareep, prepared from the highly poisonous juice of the bitter cassava plant, is a major flavoring agent in this savory stew. In Guyana, traditionally, when the meat is eaten, some of the cooking liquid is reserved to start the new pepperpot in much the same manner as a sourdough or yogurt culture is used. It is possible for visitors to today's Caribbean to taste pepperpots which go back decades.

1 ½ TABLESPOONS VEGETABLE OIL

1 POUND PORK LOIN, CUT INTO 2-INCH PIECES

2 POUNDS BEEF, CUT INTO 2-INCH PIECES

1 POUND COOKED OXTAILS, CUT INTO 2-INCH CHUNKS

1 LARGE ONION, DICED

3 CLOVES GARLIC, MINCED

¾ CUP CASSAREEP (SEE GLOSSARY)

2 BAY LEAVES

4 CLOVES

6 WIRI WIRI—TYPE CHILES

SERVES 6 TO 8   In a large saucepan, heat the oil and brown the meat, onion, and garlic. Add the remaining ingredients and water to cover. Bring the mixture to a slow boil, lower the heat, cover, and continue to cook for 2 hours.

MODONGO

Tripe is not everyone's dish; however, those who enjoy it in a spicy stew will enjoy this Puerto Rican version. Here the traditional onion, tomato, bell pepper, and garlic mixture of the sofrito subtly lends its flavor to the tripe and creates a dish that even nontripe eaters might want to attempt.

1½ POUNDS PRECOOKED TRIPE

2 TABLESPOONS FRESHLY
   SQUEEZED LIME JUICE

¼ CUP SOFRITO (PAGE 120)

1 QUART WATER

1 CUP COOKED AND DRAINED
   GARBANZO BEANS (CHICK-
   PEAS), FRESH OR CANNED

SALT, FRESHLY GROUND BLACK
   PEPPER, AND FRESH CHILE TO
   TASTE

4 MEDIUM-SIZE POTATOES,
   PEELED AND HALVED

½ POUND CALABAZA, PEELED AND
   CUT INTO 1-INCH DICE

SERVES 6   The precooked tripe that you purchase from your butcher should have been cleaned thoroughly. However, when at home, wash the tripe well with the lime juice. Place it in a saucepan and boil it for 5 minutes. Drain, and cut it into small pieces.

Place the tripe into a large saucepan with the sofrito, water, garbanzo beans, and seasonings and cook over low heat until the tripe is fork tender, about 25 minutes. Add the potatoes and pumpkin and continue to cook for 10 minutes until they are done. Serve with white rice.

ROPA VIEJA

Ropa vieja ("old clothes" in Spanish) was a traditional way to serve leftover roasts in old Cuba. The tomatoes, garlic, onions, and green peppers that form so much of the traditional seasoning of Spanish America are found here. This is traditionally served with French-fried potatoes.

2 POUNDS LEFTOVER POT ROAST

2 TEASPOONS SALT

FRESHLY GROUND BLACK PEPPER
  TO TASTE

2 CLOVES GARLIC, MINCED

3 TABLESPOONS VEGETABLE OIL

2 MEDIUM-SIZE ONIONS, CHOPPED

2 MEDIUM-SIZE TOMATOES,
  PEELED, SEEDED, AND
  CHOPPED

2 MEDIUM-SIZE GREEN BELL
  PEPPERS, SEEDED AND
  CHOPPED

1 TABLESPOON CAPERS

SERVES 8   Shred the meat into strips and season it with the salt, pepper, and garlic.

In a large heavy skillet, heat the oil and brown the onions, tomatoes, nd bell peppers for 5 minutes over medium heat, stirring occasionally. ʌdd the meat and capers. Lower the heat and continue to cook for 10 ıinutes. Serve hot.

CURRY GOAT

This dish is a legacy of the culinary mixing of the Caribbean. India's curry spices up the goat meat that is an island staple. In the States, goat meat can be found in butcher ships in Caribbean neighborhoods or in Greek neighborhoods. If you're squeamish about using goat meat, substitute mutton.

2 POUNDS GOAT OR MUTTON, CUT INTO 1-INCH CUBES

1 CLOVE GARLIC, MINCED

2 LARGE TOMATOES, PEELED, SEEDED, AND COARSELY CHOPPED

2 MEDIUM-SIZE ONIONS, CHOPPED

1 SCALLION, INCLUDING GREEN TOP, MINCED

1 SHALLOT, MINCED

1 SCOTCH BONNET—TYPE CHILE, SEEDED AND MINCED

3 TABLESPOONS MADRAS-TYPE CURRY POWDER

SALT AND FRESHLY GROUND BLACK PEPPER TO TASTE

2 TABLESPOONS BUTTER

¼ CUP VEGETABLE OIL FOR FRYING

2½ CUPS WATER

SERVES 4 TO 6   Place the meat in a large bowl and add the garlic, tomatoes, onions, scallion, shallot, chile, curry powder, salt and pepper. Mix them together well and allow the meat to marinate for at least 30 minutes.

Heat the butter and oil in a large skillet. Remove the meat from the marinade, reserving the marinade, and brown the cubes in the skillet. Add the marinade, then the water. Cover and cook over medium heat for 1¼ hours, or until the meat is tender. Taste for seasoning and serve over white rice.

JAMBON GLACÉ

This is the classic Martiniquaise Christmas dish. It serves as a centerpiece for the réveillon dinner that is attended by the whole family after midnight mass. The baked ham is made extra special by its burnt brown sugar glaze. You can prepare it either from the traditional country ham or from the precooked hams that are currently on the market.

1 5- TO 7-POUND SMOKED HAM, BUTT END

1 CUP DARK BROWN SUGAR

½ CUP DARK MARTINIQUE RUM

PINEAPPLE SLICES AND CANDIED CHERRIES FOR GARNISH (OPTIONAL)

SERVES 10   Preheat the oven to 425°. Remove the skin from the ham, if still on, by slipping a sharp knife under it and slicing it off. Trim the fat down to half an inch, if necessary. Place the ham in a roasting pan and place it in the oven. Lower the heat to 325° and cook the ham for approximately 20 minutes per pound.

Mix the brown sugar and rum well. Remove the ham from the oven and cover it with the glaze. Raise the oven heat to 425° again and allow the glaze to caramelize. Serve at once. You may wish to decorate the ham with pineapple slices and candied cherries after you put on the glaze.

SANCOCHO

In this classic Dominican stew the vegetables may include anything from cassava to plantain to even green figs; meats can be everything from stewing beef to calf's head. The flavor comes from a traditional Hispanic seasoning known as a recaito, which is the Hispanic Caribbean's answer to Barbados's Seasoning (page 118). Sancocho is traditionally served with white rice, although it's almost a meal in itself.

¾ POUND SALT PORK, CUT INTO ½-
   INCH CUBES

1 TABLESPOON BUTTER

2 SPRIGS PARSLEY, MINCED

2 SPRIGS CORIANDER, MINCED

1 TABLESPOON MINCED GREEN
   BELL PEPPER

1 TABLESPOON MINCED LEEK

1 TEASPOON MINCED SCOTCH
   BONNET—TYPE CHILE

SALT AND FRESHLY GROUND
   BLACK PEPPER TO TASTE

2 GREEN PLANTAINS, PEELED AND
   CUT INTO 2-INCH PIECES

½ POUND OKRA, TOPPED, TAILED,
   AND CUT INTO 1-INCH PIECES

½ POUND SWEET POTATOES,
   PEELED AND COARSELY DICED

¼ POUND SWEET CASSAVA,
   PEELED AND COARSELY DICED

1 QUART WATER

SERVES 4 TO 6   Place the salt pork in a bowl of water to soak. After 30 minutes discard the water and replace it with fresh water; soak for another 30 minutes.

Heat the butter in a large saucepan and fry the minced parsley, coriander, green pepper, leek, chile, and salt and pepper in it over medium heat to form the seasoning known as a recaito. Add the meat, cut-up vegetables, and water to the saucepan. Lower the heat and simmer for 1 hour, or until all of the vegetables are soft. Serve hot in bowls with white rice.

SAUTÉED LIVER
CREOLE-STYLE

Liver with onions is not everyone's favorite dish. But for those who are aficionados, this liver prepared in the creole manner with garlic, red wine, chile, thyme, parsley, and onion is nothing short of ambrosial.

1 POUND CALF'S LIVER, VEINS
   AND MEMBRANES REMOVED
FRESHLY GROUND BLACK PEPPER
   TO TASTE
1 CLOVE GARLIC, MINCED
1 TEASPOON MINCED SCOTCH
   BONNET—TYPE CHILE
1 BRANCH FRESH THYME,
   CRUSHED, OR ¼ TEASPOON
   DRIED

¼ CUP RED WINE
2 TABLESPOONS OLIVE OIL
2 TABLESPOONS BUTTER
1 LARGE ONION, THINLY SLICED
¼ CUP FLOUR

SERVES 4   Wash the liver and cut it into 1-inch pieces. Place the black pepper, garlic, chile, thyme, red wine, and olive oil into a glass bowl and whisk it until the ingredients are well mixed. Place the liver pieces into this marinade and let them sit, covered, for 1 hour. Heat the butter in a heavy skillet, add the onion, and cook until golden but not browned. Remove the liver pieces from the marinade, drain them, and coat them with the flour. Sauté them rapidly on either side until they have reached the desired doneness. Adjust seasoning (no salt, please, before this point!) and serve hot with white rice.

POULET LANTERNE

La Lanterne was a wonderful restaurant in the hills above Pétionville near Port-au-Prince, where the Swiss chef and his charming Haitian wife used to receive one and all with typically warm Haitian hospitality. One of the specialties of the house was Poulet Bruno. Unfortunately, the recipe disappeared with the restaurant. Here, then, is my version.

1 3- TO 4-POUND FRYING
   CHICKEN, CUT INTO SERVING
   PIECES
3 TABLESPOONS SALTED BUTTER
2 TEASPOONS BELL'S POULTRY
   SEASONING
SALT AND FRESHLY GROUND
   BLACK PEPPER TO TASTE

1 CUP CRUSHED FRESH
   PINEAPPLE
1 TABLESPOON DIJON-STYLE
   MUSTARD
½ CUP FRESHLY GRATED COCONUT

SERVES 4 TO 6   Preheat the oven to 350°. Wash the chicken parts and place them in a baking pan. Dot pieces of butter over the chicken and sprinkle it with the poultry seasoning, salt and pepper. Place the chicken in the oven and bake for 20 minutes.

Remove the chicken from the oven, pour off the pan juices, and reserve them in a small bowl. Add the pineapple and mustard to the pan juices and stir. Cover the chicken pieces with half of the mixture and return them to the oven for 15 minutes, basting frequently with the remaining sauce. Remove the chicken from the oven.

Heat the broiler. Sprinkle the coconut over the top of the chicken and place it under the broiler. Cook until the coconut has browned, about 3 minutes. Serve at once.

CHICHARRÓN DE POLLO

Chicharrón de pollo, tasty bite-size pieces of chicken marinated in a rum and soy sauce, are so popular in the Dominican Republic that they should be considered the national dish. They are found on everything from menus at small local restaurants to room service menus at fancy resorts.

1 2- TO 3-POUND FRYING CHICKEN

¼ CUP FRESHLY SQUEEZED LIME
  JUICE

1 TABLESPOON GINGER SOY
  SAUCE

SALT TO TASTE

1 ½ CUPS VEGETABLE OIL FOR
  FRYING

1 CUP FLOUR

½ TEASPOON PAPRIKA

FRESHLY GROUND BLACK PEPPER
  TO TASTE

LEMON SLICES FOR GARNISH

SERVES 4 TO 6   Clean the chicken and cut it into 16 small pieces by dividing the wings, thighs, breasts, and legs into halves.

Prepare a marinade from the lime juice, soy sauce, and salt and place the chicken pieces in the marinade. Cover and refrigerate for at least 5 hours.

When ready to cook, heat the oil to 325° in a heavy cast-iron skillet. Place the flour, paprika, and salt and pepper in a brown paper bag. Add the chicken pieces a few at a time. Shake them to coat with the flour and seasoning mixture and then fry for about 6 minutes on each side, or until golden brown. Do not fry too many pieces at once as the oil will cool and the frying will take longer.

Serve the chicharrón hot, garnished with the lemon slices. Diners will squirt lemon juice on the chicken bits to enhance the flavor.

ASOPAO DE POLLO

This is Puerto Rico's take on Spain's paella. Here rice and chicken team up with ham, olives, capers, tomatoes, and, of course, garlic to make a soupy stew that is savored all over the island.

1 2- TO 3-POUND FRYING CHICKEN

SALT TO TASTE

1 TEASPOON DRIED OREGANO

1 CLOVE GARLIC, MINCED

2 TABLESPOONS LARD

⅓ CUP DICED COOKED HAM

1 MEDIUM-SIZE ONION, DICED

2 MEDIUM-SIZE TOMATOES, DICED

1 MEDIUM-SIZE GREEN BELL
    PEPPER, DICED

1 ½ QUARTS WATER

1 TABLESPOON CAPERS

¼ CUP DICED PIMENTO-STUFFED
    OLIVES

2 CUPS UNCOOKED RICE

1 CUP COOKED PEAS, FOR
    GARNISH

4 PIMENTOS, CUT INTO JULIENNE
    STRIPS, FOR GARNISH

½ CUP FRESHLY GRATED
    PARMESAN CHEESE

SERVES 6 TO 8   Wash the chicken and cut it into serving pieces. Mix the salt, oregano, and garlic together and rub it onto the chicken pieces.

Heat the lard in a heavy saucepan. Brown the chicken in the lard and then add the diced ham, onion, tomatoes, and green pepper. Lower the heat, cover the saucepan, and simmer the mixture for 30 minutes.

Remove the pan from the heat; when the chicken is cool enough to handle, remove the meat from the bones, and replace it in the pot. Add the water, capers, and olives and cook for 5 minutes. Add the rice, stir, and simmer until the rice is tender but still slightly moist.

Serve at once, garnished with the cooked peas and pimento strips, and sprinkled with the Parmesan cheese. The asopao must be served immediately, otherwise it will lose its characteristic soupiness.

SALT ROASTED

CHICKEN

In many parts of the Caribbean, as in the southern United States, chicken is the traditional festive dish. Friends speak about childhood memories of chickens being chased around yards and rapidly dispatched to serve as the main course at everything from weddings to wakes. Salt roasted chicken preserves the juices of the chicken by transforming the skin into a crispy crust of salt, pepper, and poultry seasoning.

1 3- TO 4-POUND ROASTING CHICKEN	2 TEASPOONS BELL'S POULTRY SEASONING
3 TABLESPOONS BUTTER	1 MEDIUM-SIZE ONION
1 TABLESPOON FRESHLY SQUEEZED LIME JUICE	CHUTNEY (SEE SAUCES, CONDIMENTS, AND
1 TABLESPOON SALT	SEASONINGS)
1½ TEASPOONS FRESHLY GROUND BLACK PEPPER	

SERVES 4 TO 6   Preheat the oven to 450°. Wash the chicken, burn off any pin feathers, and place it in a roasting pan. Cut half of the butter into small pieces and, gently lifting the skin of the chicken breast, place most of them between the skin and the flesh. Reserve a few bits for the body cavity of the chicken.

Heat the other half of the butter in a small saucepan with the lime juice. Pour the butter and lime juice mixture over the chicken. Prepare a mixture of the salt, pepper, and poultry seasoning and rub it all over the chicken, reserving a bit. Peel the onion and rub it with the reserved seasoning mixture. Place it in the chicken's body cavity. Place the chicken in the oven and cook for 5 minutes. Reduce the heat to 350° and bake for 40 minutes. Do not baste the chicken, as the skin will become crackling crisp, but check occasionally to see that it is browning nicely. Serve hot with chutneys as accompaniment.

BAJAN FRIED CHICKEN

The wonders that the cooks of Baxter's Road work with fish (page 179), they also work with fried chicken. The secret is in the seasoning.

1 2½- TO 3-POUND FRYING CHICKEN, CUT INTO PIECES	½ CUP FLOUR
2 CUPS VEGETABLE OIL FOR FRYING	1 TABLESPOON CORNMEAL
¼ CUP OR MORE SEASONING (PAGE 118)	2 TEASPOONS BELL'S POULTRY SEASONING
	SALT AND FRESHLY GROUND BLACK PEPPER TO TASTE

SERVES 6   Wash and clean the chicken pieces and pat them dry on paper towels. Heat the oil to 375° in a heavy skillet. With a sharp knife, score the chicken pieces and fill each slash with a bit of seasoning, poking to ensure that it is well inside the chicken. Mix the flour, cornmeal, Bell's Seasoning, salt and pepper in a paper bag. Place the chicken pieces in the bag and shake until they are well coated. Place the chicken pieces in the hot oil and cook for 20 to 25 minutes, turning occasionally to ensure that they are golden brown on all sides. Remove the chicken from the oil and drain it on paper towels. Serve hot.

BUCKRA TURKEY
À LA LARRY

Larry Bailey, a good friend, lives out in the country near Kingston. One year, he was taken with the idea of raising turkeys for the holidays for his friends. The chicks were purchased, the appropriate houses were constructed, and the turkeys began to grow. Imagine everyone's surprise when, rather than the familiar brownish bewattled birds, Larry's turkeys turned out to be all white. Hence the genesis of Buckra Turkey à la Larry. (Buckra or bakra means white or white-identified in Jamaican patois.)

1 8-POUND TURKEY, WITH
  GIBLETS RESERVED
¼ CUP FRESHLY SQUEEZED LIME
  JUICE
¾ CUP (1½ STICKS) BUTTER
4 CUPS FRESH BREAD CRUMBS
¼ CUP MANIOC FLOUR
1 TABLESPOON BELL'S POULTRY
  SEASONING

SALT AND FRESHLY GROUND
  BLACK PEPPER TO TASTE
2 TEASPOONS MINCED SHALLOTS
1 MEDIUM-SIZE ONION, MINCED
2 STALKS CELERY, MINCED
¼ CUP DARK JAMAICAN RUM

SERVES 8 TO 10   Clean the turkey well and rub it inside and out with half of the lime juice. Cut half of the butter into small pieces and, gently lifting the skin between the breast and the flesh, dot the pieces all over the turkey flesh.

Prepare a dressing from the remaining dry ingredients and vegetables. Mix the remaining lime juice and the rum together and add them to the dry dressing, mixing them through with your hands. Loosely place the dressing in the turkey's body and neck cavities. Do not pack it too tightly as it will expand while cooking. Truss the bird and place it in a large roasting pan. Melt the remaining butter and pour it over the turkey. Place the turkey in the oven and cook it for approximately 3½ hours, basting it with pan juices every 15 minutes. Serve with Pineapple Chutney (page 111) as accompaniment.

CURRIED CHICKEN

Trinidad's curries, like their Guyanese counterparts, have their origins in the waves of immigrants from southern India who found their way to the Caribbean in the post-slavery period. Like all previous immigrants from Europe and Africa, they brought their culinary knowledge with them. In the Caribbean, the curry that was a mainstay in India has become a snack. Yes, it still turns up gracing the tables of such restaurants as Trinidad's venerable Mangal's, but it is also available on the streets, served wrapped in a crepelike bread known as *roti* (page 202).

3 TABLESPOONS BUTTER

1 LARGE ONION, MINCED

3 CLOVES GARLIC, MINCED

2 TEASPOONS MINCED FRESH
GINGER

3 TABLESPOONS MADRAS-TYPE
CURRY POWDER

½ TEASPOON CRUSHED RED
CHILES

½ CUP OR MORE CANE VINEGAR

3 POUNDS SKINLESS, BONELESS
CHICKEN BREASTS, CUT INTO
STRIPS

4 LARGE POTATOES, PEELED AND
CHOPPED

SERVES 4 TO 6 In a large frying pan, heat the butter and sauté the onion, garlic, and ginger until the onion is soft, but not brown. Add the curry powder and chiles, stirring so that they do not stick or burn. Add the vinegar. There should be enough to make a smooth paste. (You may need up to ¼ cup more.)

Cover the chicken pieces with the paste and place them in a covered bowl in the refrigerator. Allow the chicken pieces to marinate for at least 2 hours. When ready to cook, place the chicken pieces in a large frying pan and add enough water to reconstitute the paste and prevent scorching. Cover and cook over low heat for 30 minutes. (You may find that you will have to add more water to prevent scorching.) After 30 minutes, add the potatoes, cover, and continue to cook for an additional 15 minutes, or until the potatoes and chicken are done. Serve with Mango Chutney (page 112), chopped peanuts, raisins, and freshly grated coconut as a fancy dinner, or with roti as a snack.

CHINESE ROAST
CHICKEN

The Asian presence in the Caribbean is little heralded by scholars. Yet, in countries like Jamaica, Trinidad, and Guadeloupe, it has been a steady influence on things culinary. Kitchen larders are apt to have any number of Asian staples, which are then incorporated into the daily repertoire with astonishing results. In Kingston's supermarkets, it is possible to find numerous varieties of sauces: oyster sauce, hoisin sauce, duck sauce, multiple varieties of soy sauce, as well as other ingredients that are unknown outside of ethnic establishments even in urban supermarkets in the States. Chinese roast chicken grew out of a discussion that I had with Averile Bodden, the owner of a Jamaican supermarket, whose Jamaican patois would convince even the most skeptical of her Jamaican-ness and whose look brings to mind imperial China. She divulged the secret of the Chinese roast chickens in her store's meat chest . . . egg powder.

1 4- TO 5-POUND ROASTING CHICKEN

1 TEASPOON RICE WINE

2 TABLESPOONS LIGHT SOY SAUCE

1 TEASPOON SUGAR

1 TABLESPOON EGG POWDER (SEE GLOSSARY)

2 TABLESPOONS UNSALTED BUTTER

1 MEDIUM-SIZE ONION, PEELED

SERVES 4 TO 6   Preheat the oven to 450°. Wash the chicken. Prepare a marinade of the rice wine, soy sauce, and sugar and coat the chicken with it inside and out. Dust the egg powder over the chicken. Cut the butter into small pieces and place it between the skin and the flesh of the breast and inside the chicken's body cavity; then insert the onion into the cavity.

   Place the chicken in a roasting pan and into the oven. Reduce the heat to 350° and cook the chicken for 1 hour, basting occasionally with pan juices. Serve hot with rice and peas and accompanied by one of the chutneys in the chapter Sauces, Condiments, and Seasonings, for a multicultural Caribbean meal.

CROQUETAS DE POLLO

Fried foods are extremely popular in the Caribbean in general and in Puerto Rico in particular. The range is astonishing and they appear on lunch and dinner tables and as appetizers and cocktail snacks. These chicken croquettes can be made large and served for lunch or dinner, or reduced in size and used as appetizers.

2 POUNDS SKINLESS, BONELESS
   CHICKEN BREASTS

3 TABLESPOONS BUTTER

½ CUP FLOUR

1 TEASPOON SALT, PLUS EXTRA TO
   TASTE

¼ TEASPOON FRESHLY GROUND
   BLACK PEPPER

1 ½ CUPS CHICKEN BROTH

1 TABLESPOON GRATED ONION

¼ TEASPOON MINCED SCOTCH
   BONNET—TYPE CHILE

LARD OR VEGETABLE OIL FOR
   FRYING

3 EGGS, BEATEN

1 ½ CUPS DRY BREAD CRUMBS

MAKES ABOUT 5 LARGE OR 10 SMALL CROQUETTES
Place the chicken breasts in a saucepan, cover with water, cover, and cook over low heat until tender. When the chicken is cooked, grind it in a food processor until it is well minced.

Melt the butter in a saucepan and add the flour, 1 teaspoon salt, pepper, and chicken broth to it, stirring until it becomes a thick sauce. Remove the sauce from the heat and allow it to cool. Fold the onion, chile, and chicken into the sauce, making sure that it is well mixed.

Meanwhile, heat 3 inches of oil or lard for frying to 375° in a heavy saucepan or deep-fat fryer. Beat the eggs and salt together in a bowl. Shape the chicken mixture into croquettes using 2 tablespoons. Dip the croquettes into bread crumbs, then into the egg mixture, and again into the bread crumbs. Fry for about 3 minutes on each side, or until golden brown. Drain and serve hot.

FRICASSEED CHICKEN

Kittian Kitchen at the Golden Lemon sells all sorts of homemade spices and teas. It was there, in discussion with one of the salespeople, that I discovered the recipe for this fricasseed chicken, on which I have elaborated. The ginger, garlic, scallions, and Scotch Bonnet chile all work together to give this dish a truly Caribbean flavor.

1 4- TO 5-POUND CHICKEN, CUT INTO SERVING PIECES

3 MEDIUM-SIZE ONIONS, 1 SLICED, 2 CHOPPED

3 SCALLIONS, INCLUDING THE GREEN TOPS, CHOPPED

SALT AND FRESHLY GROUND BLACK PEPPER TO TASTE

1 1-INCH PIECE OF FRESH GINGER, MINCED

½ CUP VEGETABLE OIL FOR FRYING

3 MEDIUM-SIZE TOMATOES, PEELED, SEEDED, AND COARSELY CHOPPED

1 CLOVE GARLIC, MINCED

1 SCOTCH BONNET—TYPE CHILE, PRICKED WITH A FORK

½ TEASPOON PAPRIKA

2 TABLESPOONS HOT WATER

SERVES 6   The night before cooking, wash the chicken parts and pat them dry. Mix the sliced onion with the scallions, salt and pepper, and ginger. Rub the mixture over the chicken parts. Cover and refrigerate overnight.

When ready to cook, remove the seasonings from the chicken and wipe it dry. Heat the oil in a heavy skillet and brown the chicken on all sides. Pour off most of the remaining cooking oil and add the chopped onions and remaining ingredients, adding salt to taste. Lower the heat, cover, and allow to simmer for about 45 minutes, or until the chicken is fork tender, adding a bit of water from time to time so that the mixture remains slightly moist. Serve hot with peas and rice.

FONDUE MARINIÈRE

It is almost impossible to get a bad meal in Guadeloupe. French cooking along with a fiery dose of African culinary know-how combine to make the island a gourmet's delight. At Les Oiseaux, chef Arthur Rolle, a Guadeloupean man with eyes of sea-foam blue, breaks with an island tradition by which women are the best creole chefs. At his restaurant, he serves traditional dishes such as *féroce d'avocat* and innovative dishes such as this *fondue marinière,* a contemporary dish that will allow you to use that fondue set that has been sitting in the back of your kitchen cupboard since 1975.

2 CUPS COCONUT OIL

2 CUPS PEANUT OIL

1 POUND RED SNAPPER, CUT INTO
   1-INCH PIECES

1 POUND KINGFISH OR WHITING
   FILETS, CUT INTO 1-INCH
   PIECES

1 POUND FRESH TUNA, CUT INTO
   1-INCH PIECES

2 SWEET POTATOES, PEELED AND
   CUT INTO 1-INCH PIECES

SERVES 6   Place the coconut and peanut oils into the fondue pot and bring them to a boil over a medium flame. Place the fondue pot on the fondue burner. Arrange portions of the fish on individual plates along with the dipping sauces and serve. Any of the hot sauce recipes in the chapter Sauces, Condiments, and Seasonings may also be used as dipping sauces. Proceed as for any fondue.

DIPPING SAUCE #1

1 RIPE AVOCADO   ½ CUP MAYONNAISE

½ SCOTCH BONNET—TYPE CHILE,

 MINCED

Peel the avocado, cut it into chunks, and place it and the chile in a food processor and mix until a fine paste. Add the paste to the mayonnaise mixture. Chill and serve.

DIPPING SAUCE #2

¼ CUP GREEN PEPPERCORN ½ CUP MAYONNAISE

 MUSTARD

Mix the mustard and mayonnaise together. Chill and serve.

LAMBI CREOLE

Lambi, or conch, is one of the Caribbean's seafoods that has mythic properties. Its meat is considered to be a "restorative" and an aphrodisiac in the Bahamas. Its shell, called an *abeng* in Jamaica, was used by the Maroons to signal their uprisings. The shell is found on the altars for the Yoruba goddess of salt water and motherhood, Yemaya, in Cuba and Puerto Rico; and its haunting notes are heard in Haitian voodoo ceremonies to Agoué, the loa of the briny deep. In today's Haiti, a suburb of Port-au-Prince is known as Lambi because so many conch are fished there. A club on the main street boasts a wall made of conch shells and features conch dishes and great music, a heady Caribbean combination.

1 POUND CONCH MEAT, FRESH,
   CANNED, OR FROZEN
JUICE OF 2 LEMONS
2 TABLESPOONS BUTTER
1 SMALL ONION, CHOPPED
1 CLOVE GARLIC, CHOPPED
2 BIRD PEPPER—TYPE CHILES,
   CHOPPED

2 TABLESPOONS WATER
2 MEDIUM-SIZE TOMATOES,
   PEELED, SEEDED, AND
   COARSELY CHOPPED
1 SPRIG FRESH THYME
SALT AND FRESHLY GROUND
   BLACK PEPPER TO TASTE

SERVES 2   Tenderize the conch meat by beating it with a mallet for 15 minutes; then wash it thoroughly with water and the lemon juice until the oily feel of the meat is gone. Cut the conch into small pieces.

In a skillet, heat the butter and sauté the onion, garlic, and chile. Add the conch and remaining ingredients and cook until tender. Serve with white rice.

FRIED FISH

BAXTER'S

ROAD

Baxter's Road is a slightly disreputable street in Bridgetown, Barbados. Most tourists to the island never get near it during the day and certainly don't see it at night. However, any Bajan will tell you that if you want to taste some of the best fried fish in the area, head to Baxter's Road after the sun goes down. Then, large ladies with commanding voices and thick arms tend iron pots where they fry chicken and fish and create an African street market right in the middle of Barbados's capital. The women's dexterity as they score the fish that is so fresh it is almost flip-flopping in the pail, add the mossy green seasoning, and pop it into the bubbling fat is a testimony to Africa's culinary gifts to the Caribbean.

4 DOLPHIN STEAKS (SEE NOTE)

JUICE OF 2 LIMES

VEGETABLE OIL FOR FRYING

1 EGG

2 TABLESPOONS MILK

¼ CUP SEASONING (PAGE 118)

½ CUP FLOUR

½ CUP DRY BREAD CRUMBS

SERVES 4   Rub the fish steaks with the lime juice. Heat 2 inches of oil to 375° in a heavy skillet or cauldron.

Meanwhile, beat the egg and milk together in a small bowl. Score the fish steaks next to the center bone and on each side; place a bit of the seasoning in the slits. (Use about 1 tablespoon of seasoning per fish steak.) Dredge the steaks in flour, dip them in milk and egg, and cover them with bread crumbs. Fry for 5 minutes or more, turning to make sure that each side is golden. Drain on absorbent paper and serve hot.

NOTE • *Don't use Flipper but the fish that is also known as dorado or mahi. Whole porgies can be substituted.*

STEAMED FISH

Steamed fish is found on numerous Caribbean islands. Indeed, steamed fish is a misnomer, as the fish is first sautéed and then steamed. The dish is served with funghi in the U.S. Virgin Islands, with bammie in Jamaica, and is a favorite lunchtime special on small dockside restaurants in places like French Town in Saint Thomas and Port Royal, Jamaica.

6 SMALL RED SNAPPERS,
  CLEANED AND READY FOR
  COOKING

½ CUP CIDER VINEGAR

1 TABLESPOON SALT, PLUS EXTRA
  TO TASTE

2 TEASPOONS MINCED SCOTCH
  BONNET—TYPE CHILE, PLUS 1
  WHOLE CHILE

JUICE OF 2 LIMES, PLUS AN
  EXTRA SQUEEZE

½ CUP FLOUR

½ CUP VEGETABLE OIL FOR
  FRYING

1 MEDIUM-SIZE ONION, MINCED

2 SPRIGS FRESH THYME OR ½
  TEASPOON DRIED

FRESHLY GROUND BLACK PEPPER
  TO TASTE

2 MEDIUM-SIZE TOMATOES,
  PEELED, SEEDED, AND
  COARSELY CHOPPED

3 CUPS WATER

SERVES 6   Wash the fish in a mixture of salted water and vinegar. Score the fish diagonally from head to tail. Mix the salt and the minced chile pepper together into a paste and place a bit of it into the slits in the fish. Cover the fish with the lime juice and allow it to sit for at least 1 hour.

Remove the fish from the marinade and dry it off. Roll it in the flour and shake off the excess. Heat the oil in a heavy skillet. Place the fish in the oil and fry it over medium heat until golden brown; remove the fish and set it aside. Add the onion, thyme, whole chile, salt and pepper to the oil and cook until the onion is light brown, stirring occasionally. Add the tomatoes and cook until the mixture becomes a thick sauce. Add the water and bring the sauce to a boil. Lower the heat and continue to cook for about 5 minutes. Add the fish and cook for an additional 5 minutes, turning the fish once. Just before removing, add a squeeze of lime juice and stir once. Serve with white rice, bammie, or peas and rice.

MATÉTÉ CRABES

This dish is a descendant of ago glain, a dish from the former kingdom of Dahomey in West Africa. On Easter Monday and on the Monday following Pentecost, families in the French-speaking Caribbean flock to the beaches for picnics, when matété crabes is the dish traditionally served. If you see matoutou crabs on the menu, don't despair. When the dish is made with manioc flour instead of white rice it takes this name.

3 QUARTS WATER

6 LIVE 1-POUND CRABS

2 TABLESPOONS UNSALTED
    BUTTER

2 TABLESPOONS LIGHT OLIVE OIL

1 CLOVE GARLIC, SLICED

1 ONION, MINCED

1 SCALLION, INCLUDING THE
    GREEN TOP, MINCED

3 CHIVES, MINCED

1 SPRIG PARSLEY, MINCED

1 BRANCH FRESH THYME,
    MINCED, OR ¼ TEASPOON DRIED

¾ CUP BOILING WATER

1 BAY LEAF

SALT AND FRESHLY GROUND
    BLACK PEPPER TO TASTE

JUICE OF 1 LIME

1 SCOTCH BONNET—TYPE CHILE,
    SEEDED AND MINCED

3 CUPS COOKED RICE

SERVES 6   Bring the 3 quarts of water to a boil in a large saucepan or stockpot. Place the live crabs in the boiling water and cook them for 10 minutes. Drain the crabs and cut them into small pieces, removing as much of the broken shells as possible.

In a large skillet, heat the butter and oil and add the garlic, onion, scallion, chives, parsley, and thyme. Add the crab pieces and cook for about 10 minutes, or until they are lightly browned. Moisten the mixture with the boiling water, add the bay leaf, salt and pepper, lime juice, and chile. Cook over a low flame for 15 to 20 minutes, or until the mixture forms a thick sauce. Serve mixed with the rice. Be sure to warn your guests about possible crab shell bits and let them know that to truly savor matété crabes, they must use their fingers.

PISQUETTES

This treat is not available all year round, but will delight you if you're lucky enough to be in the Caribbean. Pisquettes are tiny fish found in Haiti and in Martinique; they are known by the poetic name of ti-ti-ri in Guadeloupe. No one is sure whether they are dwarf fish or simply young fish, but whatever they are, they're delicious served up in omelettes or fritters or simply fried. The best substitute for pisquettes is whitebait.

VEGETABLE OIL FOR FRYING

1 POUND WHITEBAIT

JUICE OF 1 LEMON

½ CUP FLOUR

SALT AND FRESHLY GROUND

BLACK PEPPER TO TASTE

¼ TEASPOON BELL'S POULTRY

SEASONING

SERVES 1   Heat 3 inches of oil to 375° in a heavy cast-iron skillet. Wash the fish in the lemon juice and dry thoroughly. Place the flour and seasonings in a brown paper bag, add the fish, and shake them until they are coated with the flour and seasoning mixture. Fry the fish in the hot oil for 3 to 5 minutes, until they are crisp. Drain on absorbent paper towels and serve hot.

SHRIMP CREOLE

This much-imitated and much-abused dish probably has as many variations as there are cooks in the Caribbean. This version uses the traditional
Caribbean seasonings of fresh thyme, scallions, chives, tomatoes, garlic,
and onions as well as green peppers and chile.

3 TABLESPOONS BUTTER

1 CLOVE GARLIC, MINCED

1 TEASPOON MINCED FRESH
GINGER

1 SCALLION, INCLUDING THE
GREEN TOP, MINCED

2 CHIVES, MINCED

1 SMALL ONION, MINCED

2 BRANCHES FRESH THYME OR ½
TEASPOON DRIED

1 SMALL GREEN BELL PEPPER,
MINCED

3 POUNDS RAW SHRIMP, SHELLED
AND DEVEINED

3 MEDIUM-SIZE TOMATOES,
PEELED, SEEDED, AND
COARSELY CHOPPED

2 TEASPOONS MINCED SCOTCH
BONNET—TYPE CHILE OR TO
TASTE

SERVES 6   Heat the butter in a heavy frying pan. Add the garlic,
ginger, scallion, chives, onion, thyme, and green pepper and sauté until
the onion is slightly browned. Add the shrimp, tomatoes, and chile. Cover
and cook over a medium flame for 15 minutes, stirring occasionally and
adding water if the mixture becomes too dry. Serve hot with white rice.

COURT BOUILLON
ANTILLAIS

The court bouillon of the French-speaking Caribbean differs radically from its European counterpart. The latter is a rich stock in which fish is traditionally poached. In the Caribbean, however, the name includes not only the poaching liquid, but also the final dish itself. The following recipe is an adaptation of the classic Antillean dish as it is prepared in Martinique's Manoir de Beauregard, a charming old manor house filled with antique furniture and brimming with atmosphere. There, if you are of a mind and the kitchen is not too busy, it is possible to watch as the dish is prepared. The kitchen is as classically Caribbean as the dish, with one wall open to the sunshine and only a few implements. The chef moves around her kitchen reaching, seasoning, and slicing with such rapidity that she seems to be a multiarmed Creole goddess of the hearth. In no time the court bouillon is ready. You leave the kitchen brimming with admiration for the Antillean tradition of transforming the ordinary into the extraordinary with a deft touch of the hand.

JUICE OF 3 LIMES

1 ½ CUPS DRY WHITE WINE

6 SMALL RED SNAPPERS, SCALED
AND CLEANED WITH THE HEADS
ON

5 CHIVES

5 SCALLIONS, INCLUDING THE
GREEN TOPS

2 MEDIUM-SIZE TOMATOES

1 MEDIUM-SIZE ONION

¼ CUP LIGHT OLIVE OIL

¾ CUP HOT WATER

1 BOUQUET GARNI: 1 BAY LEAF, 3
ALLSPICE BERRIES, AND 1
BRANCH FRESH THYME OR ¼
TEASPOON DRIED

½ SCOTCH BONNET—TYPE CHILE

SERVES 4 TO 6   Prepare a marinade from two-thirds of the lime juice and half of the white wine and marinate the fish in it for 1 to 2 hours.

Grind the chives, scallions, tomatoes, and onion together in a food processor. Heat the oil in a heavy skillet and add the ground ingredients. When the mixture has cooked for approximately 5 minutes, add the fish, lower the heat, and cook them well on both sides. Then add the hot water, the remaining white wine, bouquet garni, chile, and remaining one-third of the lime juice. Stir well and simmer the dish over low heat for 5 minutes. Serve hot with white rice.

MARTINIQUE

BLAFF

If there is such a thing as having a favorite name of a dish, blaff would win the prize hands down. The name is simply an onomatopoeia for the sound that the fish makes when it is plopped into the cooking liquid . . . blaff!

This classic dish is a personal favorite; it also appears in my previous book, *Iron Pots and Wooden Spoons: Africa's Gifts to New World Cooking.*

SALT AND FRESHLY GROUND
   BLACK PEPPER TO TASTE
6 ALLSPICE BERRIES, CRUSHED
3 CLOVES GARLIC, CRUSHED
1 SCOTCH BONNET—TYPE CHILE,
   PRICKED WITH A FORK
JUICE OF 6 LIMES
4 SMALL RED SNAPPERS, SCALED
   AND CLEANED WITH THE HEADS
   ON

1 ½ QUARTS WATER
1 SMALL ONION, SLICED
1 BOUQUET GARNI: 1 SPRIG
   FRESH THYME OR ¼ TEASPOON
   DRIED, 2 CHIVES, 1 SPRIG
   PARSLEY

SERVES 4   Prepare a marinade of the salt and pepper, half the allspice, 1 garlic clove, chile, and half the lime juice. Place the fish in a bowl, cover with the marinade, and set aside for 1 hour.

When ready to cook, place all of the remaining ingredients except the other half of lime juice and fish in a heavy pot and bring to a boil. When the water is at a rolling boil, place the fish in the liquid (listen for the blaff!) and allow it to return to the boil. Remove the fish and serve them in bowls covered with their cooking liquid and the remaining lime juice. Blaff is traditionally served with white rice.

CRASÉ DE MORUE

Écraser means "to mash" in French. This dish from Guadeloupe, an Antillean version of the Provençal aioli, allows one and all to have fun doing what Mother said never to do . . . play with one's food. Diners must make up their own "crasé" by adding the ingredients that they prefer to the sauce.

1 POUND SALTED CODFISH (SEE
   GLOSSARY)

1 BOUQUET GARNI: 1 BRANCH
   FRESH THYME OR ¼ TEASPOON
   DRIED, 2 CHIVES, 1 SCALLION,
   3 CRUSHED ALLSPICE BERRIES,
   AND ½ SCOTCH BONNET—TYPE
   CHILE

2 MEDIUM-SIZE ONIONS, SLICED

1 TEASPOON EXTRA-VIRGIN OLIVE
   OIL

1 BOK CHOY, CUT INTO 1-INCH
   PIECES

½ BREADFRUIT, PEELED, CORED,
   AND CUT INTO 1-INCH DICE, OR
   1 CUP NEW POTATOES, PEELED
   AND DICED

6 SMALL GREEN BANANAS

JUICE OF 2 LIMES, PLUS 2 LIMES
   FOR GARNISH

¼ CUP WHITE WINE VINEGAR

4 EGGS

1 RIPE AVOCADO, PEELED, PITTED,
   AND SLICED

1 SCOTCH BONNET—TYPE CHILE,
   SEEDED AND SLICED

CREOLE VINAIGRETTE (PAGE 125)

SERVES 4   Prepare the salted codfish according to the directions on page 69. Place the bouquet garni, onions, oil, and the prepared salted codfish in a stockpot and cover them with water. Slowly bring the pot to a boil over a low flame, then continue to cook for 8 minutes. Remove the codfish and keep it warm. Place the bok choy and breadfruit in the water and continue to cook until they are fork tender. Place the green bananas, unpeeled, in a separate pot and cover with water to which you have added the juice of 1 lime. When cooked, peel them and place them in a serving dish.

Meanwhile, remove the bok choy and breadfruit from the original pot and place them on a plate with the codfish, keeping them warm. Add the vinegar to the water and poach the eggs in the cooking water. While the eggs are poaching, sprinkle the avocado slices with the remaining lime juice, and arrange them on the platter with the codfish and vegetables. When the eggs are poached, remove them and place them in a separate serving dish. Serve immediately with sliced Scotch Bonnet–type chile, lime quarters, and creole vinaigrette.

The diners have a poached egg and select the additional ingredients that they wish, then mash them together with the creole vinaigrette and the hot chile in their plates.

H A I T I

GRILLED SNAPPER
LE RÉCIF

Le Récif is a marvelous seafood restaurant located on the road from Port-au-Prince to Pétionville. It is a favorite for many because rather than cope with a French menu or unfamiliar dishes, Le Récif has simplified matters by preparing an unusual menu. As diners flip through the pages, they see photographs of the ingredients and the finished dish, always prepared with the freshest fish and produce. The grilled snapper is a simple dish, but one that is a guaranteed hit at a dinner or a summer barbecue.

4 MEDIUM-SIZE RED SNAPPERS, CLEANED AND WITH THE HEADS REMOVED

¼ CUP CARIBBEAN PEPPER OIL (PAGE 117)

SERVES 4   This dish can be prepared either on an outdoor or an indoor grill. Whatever the case, heat the grill to cooking temperature. Meanwhile, score the fish on both sides and brush them with Caribbean oil. Place the fish on the grill and cook for 2 to 3 minutes on each side until done. Serve immediately.

CURRY CASCADURA

The cascadura is a local mudfish with the taste of shrimp that is found in the rivers of Trinidad. (It is called *hassah* in Guyana, where it is also found.) Local legend has it that those Trinidadian natives who eat the cascadura will return to Trinidad no matter how far from home they may roam. The legend has become widely known thanks to the story by Trinidadian writer Samuel Selvon, "Johnson and the Cascadura," and his novel *Those Who Eat the Cascadura*.

10 CASCADURA (SEE NOTE)

JUICE OF 1 LIME

1 ½ TEASPOONS SALT, PLUS EXTRA
  TO TASTE

2 TABLESPOONS MINCED FRESH
  CHIVES

¼ TEASPOON GROUND CLOVES

½ TEASPOON FRESHLY GROUND
  BLACK PEPPER OR TO TASTE

3 TABLESPOONS COCONUT OIL

5 TABLESPOONS MADRAS CURRY
  POWDER

3 OR 4 MEDIUM-SIZE TOMATOES,
  PEELED, SEEDED, AND
  COARSELY CHOPPED

2 MEDIUM-SIZE ONIONS, CHOPPED

1 ½ CUPS WATER

SERVES 4 TO 6   Wash the cascadura thoroughly with the lime juice and 1 ½ teaspoons salt. Rinse thoroughly with cold water and season them with a dry marinade prepared from the chives, cloves, black pepper, and salt.

Put the oil into a heavy cast-iron skillet and heat it over a medium flame. Add the curry powder, stirring constantly. When the curry powder is about to scorch, add the cascadura and cook over medium heat for 10 minutes, turning the fish from time to time. Add the tomatoes and onions, and when they are browned, add the water, lower the heat, and cook for 20 to 25 minutes. Serve with white rice.

NOTE ● *Frozen cascadura can be found in fish markets in West Indian neighborhoods. So now we can all be among those who eat the cascadura. Shrimp can be substituted.*

CURRIED LOBSTER
SALAD

This dish is at home served in wooden bowls on tray tables around the pool, or decorated with a chutney and served on china luncheon plates on heirloom placemats. It takes its delicate flavor from the addition of coconut cream to the dressing.

1 HEAD OF BIBB LETTUCE, WASHED, LEAVES SEPARATED

1 MEDIUM-SIZE TOMATO, SLICED

1 POUND COOKED LOBSTER TAIL MEAT

6 TABLESPOONS MAYONNAISE

½ OVERRIPE AVOCADO, PEELED AND PITTED

1 TABLESPOON COCONUT CREAM

1 TEASPOON FRESHLY SQUEEZED LIME JUICE

DASH OF RED DEVIL PEPPER SAUCE (PAGE 124)

SERVES 4   Arrange the lettuce and the tomato slices on 4 plates. Divide the cooked lobster meat on the dishes. Place the mayonnaise, avocado, coconut cream, lime juice, and hot sauce in a blender and liquefy. Pour the dressing over the salads. Serve immediately.

ESCOVEITCHED FISH

This Jamaican dish is traditionally served at Sunday morning breakfast with the fried cassava cake known as bammie. In it fried fish marinates in vinegar, allspice, onion, and Scotch Bonnet chile. Some have suggested that the dish is a combination of two culinary legacies: fried fish in the African manner meets up with the Native American method of cooking and preserving fish in a marinade (such as Mexico's ceviche). Whatever the origins, this is a dish that can be beautifully presented at a summer buffet or at a dinner party. It can be prepared a day in advance.

6 SMALL RED SNAPPERS

JUICE OF 1 LEMON

JUICE OF 2 LIMES

4 TEASPOONS SALT

4 TEASPOONS FRESHLY GROUND
  BLACK PEPPER

½ CUP VEGETABLE OIL FOR
  FRYING

2 CUPS CANE VINEGAR

1 SCOTCH BONNET—TYPE CHILE,
  CUT INTO RINGS

1 CHAYOTE, PEELED AND CUT
  INTO JULIENNE STRIPS

2 MEDIUM-SIZE ONIONS, SLICED

12 ALLSPICE BERRIES

6 WHOLE BLACK PEPPERCORNS

SERVES 6   Wash the snappers thoroughly in water to which the lemon and lime juices have been added. Dry the fish, dust them with a mixture of the salt and pepper, and set them aside.

In a skillet heat the oil to the boiling point and fry the fish on both sides until crisp, about 3 to 5 minutes per side. Remove the fish, drain it, and place it in a deep nonreactive bowl.

Prepare the marinade by placing the remaining ingredients in a small saucepan and bringing them to a boil over a medium flame about 3 minutes. Lower the heat and continue to cook until the onions are tender. Remove the marinade from the heat, cool slightly, and pour over the fish. Allow the fish to sit in the marinade for an hour to absorb all of the flavors. Serve with Bammie (page 197).

MACKEREL RUN DOWN

Run Down is another of those Jamaican dishes that was named by someone whose sense of poetry matched his or her sense of cooking. The derivation is easy. The dish goes on the stove and the mackerel is added. Then the whole thing is cooked until it runs down to a delicious dish that shows yet another way people in the Caribbean use salted and pickled fish. Run Down is often cited as one of the dishes most missed by expatriate Jamaicans.

3 POUNDS SALTED MACKEREL

2 QUARTS PLUS 1 CUP FRESHLY
MADE THICK COCONUT MILK
(PAGE 57)

1 SCOTCH BONNET—TYPE CHILE,
PRICKED WITH A FORK

2 CLOVES GARLIC, CRUSHED

6 MEDIUM-SIZE TOMATOES,
PEELED, SEEDED, AND
COARSELY CHOPPED

2 MEDIUM ONIONS, CHOPPED

3 SCALLIONS, INCLUDING GREEN
TOPS, CHOPPED

1 SHALLOT, CHOPPED

2 FRESH CHIVES, CHOPPED

3 SPRIGS FRESH THYME OR ¾
TEASPOON DRIED

2 GREEN BANANAS, PEELED AND
SLICED INTO 2-INCH PIECES

1 TEASPOON FRESHLY GROUND
BLACK PEPPER

SALT TO TASTE

SERVES 6   Place the mackerel in a bowl, cover it with water, and soak it for at least 8 hours, changing the water twice. When ready, remove fins, side bones, and heads from the fish and cut fish into pieces.

Put the coconut milk into a medium-size saucepan and bring it to a boil over high heat. When boiling, add the chile, garlic, tomatoes, onions, scallions, shallot, chives, and thyme and cook until the coconut milk begins to form a custard. Add the mackerel and cook for 5 minutes. Then add the green bananas and continue cooking until the fish is done. Add the black pepper and adjust the seasoning to taste.

BREADS

AND

BAKED

GOODS

The road from Cap Haitien to Port-au-Prince takes the traveler from Haiti's mountainous north, through the rice paddies of the central plain, past coastal sand dunes into the capital city of Port-au-Prince. Before new roads were constructed, the road would wash out during storms, leaving unwary travelers stranded. Today, the new road is passable in all weather, and has cut travel time. However, a hint of the old sense of adventure remains for all those who traveled the former route.

On my last trip, I was in for a surprise. Only a few miles outside of Cap Haitien, my driver pulled off to the side of the road. Why? I questioned. He replied, "Because this is the best place to buy *pain de kassav,* and if I don't take some home to my relatives and they find out that I have been to Cap Haitien, they will be angry." He got out of the car and approached the group of women who looked as though they could have stepped out of an eighteenth-century etching as they washed, peeled, grated, and prepared the cassava before spreading it in thin sheets on the griddles improvised from oil-drum bottoms. When the pain de kassav was cooked on one side, they adeptly flipped the large rounds over and cooked them on the other side. The negotiations—price, brownness, quantity—took some time, so that I could stroll through the small group of bakers concentrating on their task. Then, I didn't know that the bread they were making was the same bread that had sustained the Spanish colonists. I did not know that the cassava flour they were preparing dated back to pre-Columbian times and was one of the Arawaks' gifts to Caribbean cooking. All I knew was that it was a special moment: one of everyday life in the Caribbean, yet one few travelers were privileged to see. As we departed, one of the ladies came up to the car and gave me a piece of the pain de kassav to sample. The crispness of the bread with its slightly nutty taste was delicious; the flavor stayed with me all the way back to Port-au-Prince.

PAIN DE KASSAV

This is the traditional Caribbean bread. Called *pan de casabe* by the Spanish, it sustained the original colonists until they complained so much that they were sent wheat flour. The pain de kassav of Haiti and the pan de casabe of the Spanish-speaking Caribbean are thin and almost crispy.

1 POUND SWEET CASSAVA

SALT TO TASTE

2 TABLESPOONS BUTTER

(OPTIONAL)

2 CLOVES GARLIC, MINCED

(OPTIONAL)

MAKES 4 CAKES   Wash and peel the cassava tuber. Using the finest section of a grater or food processor, grate the cassava into cheesecloth. Holding the cheesecloth over the sink, squeeze to remove all of the liquid possible. Heat a heavy cast-iron skillet or griddle. Pat the cassava flour into 4 thin cakes, add salt, and fry them on the griddle until the cakes are browned on both sides.

After the cassava bread is cooked, you may wish to return them to the skillet in which you have heated the butter and the garlic. Turn each one quickly in the butter and garlic mixture for a tropical garlic bread.

CHRISTMAS CAKE

Every year, with the return of the fall season, my girl friend June Bobb from Guyana begins her citywide search for Sultanas, glacé cherries, currants, raisins, mixed lime, lemon, and orange peel, and more for her Christmas cake. Prepared months in advance so that it can marinate in high-proof rum, Christmas cake recipes are handed down from mother to daughter in families and as such are touchstones of family tradition. The baking and rum dousing only heighten the anticipation of the Christmas season when the cake is eaten with much ceremony or given away to good friends.

2 POUNDS MIXED RAISINS, PITTED PRUNES, AND CURRANTS	6 EGGS
	¼ CUP MIXED FRUIT PEEL
2 FIFTHS GUYANA OR BARBADOS RUM, OR MORE TO TASTE	½ CUP CHOPPED WALNUTS
	1 TEASPOON GROUND ALLSPICE
2⅓ CUPS DARK BROWN SUGAR	¼ TEASPOON BAKING POWDER
1 CUP BUTTER	2 CUPS FLOUR

MAKES 2 8-INCH CAKES Grind the mixed raisins, prunes, and currants in a food processor until they are a sticky paste. Pour 1 bottle of the rum over the ground dried fruit and allow it to soak for no less than 24 hours. (Many cooks let their fruit soak several months.)

Grease and doubly line two 8-inch cake pans. Preheat the oven to 300°.

Cream 1⅓ cups of the sugar and the butter; add the eggs one at a time. Add the mixed peel and walnuts to the fruit mixture and stir well.

In a heavy cast-iron skillet, caramelize the remaining cup of brown sugar until you have a dark brown liquid. After it cools slightly. but does not solidify, add ½ cup of rum. Add enough of the caramelized brown sugar and rum to the fruit and peel mixture to make it as dark as desired. Sift the dry ingredients into the fruit and peel mixture, a little at a time. Mix until a soft batter forms. If the batter is too thick, add rum to thin it. Then pour the batter into the prepared pans and bake for 1¼ hours. Test for doneness by sticking a toothpick into the center. If the cakes appear cooked (some ingredients may adhere to the toothpick, but they will be cooked), remove them from the oven. (Be careful at this point, as you do not want to overcook the cakes. If the toothpick comes out clean, your cake will be too dry.) Pour a generous amount of rum over each cake. The cakes will sizzle. As the cakes cool, continue to soak them with the rum.

When the cakes have cooled completely, remove them from the pans. If any rum remains in the pans, discard it. The cake may be covered with almond paste and then decorated with icing, but they are just as good served plain.

BAMMIE

In places like Port Royal and along the north coast of Jamaica these flat cakes are eaten with fried fish in small local restaurants. Bammie is easy to prepare but relatively time-consuming. You can shave off a few minutes by grating the sweet cassava in a food processor.

2 POUNDS SWEET CASSAVA

MAKES 1 CAKE   Peel the sweet cassava and grate it finely with a grater or food processor. Place the grated cassava in a piece of cheese-cloth and squeeze out the juice, letting the moist cassava flour remain. Place the cassava flour in a bowl and rub through it to eliminate any lumps.

Place a heavy cast-iron skillet on a low flame. When the skillet is hot, pour in the cassava flour to make a flat cake about 5 to 6 inches in diameter and ½ to ¾ inch thick. Cook until the cassava adheres and "sets." Then turn the bammie over and repeat the process on the other side. Remove from the pan and scrape to remove any scorched parts.

The bammie may be served as it is or moistened with a drop or two of milk and baked in a hot oven, browned under a grill, or fried in a skillet in bacon fat.

BULLAS

I first found out about bullas while driving into the Jamaican town of Port Antonio in the northeastern section of the island. As we rounded a corner, a sign painted on a bakery wall advertised "blessed bullas." The advertisement was impossible to ignore, and before I knew it, I was off in search of "blessed bullas." I found them; they were bagel-shaped, brown sugar and gingery-tasting hard cookies that hovered on the borderline between cookie and cracker. They were a traditional after-school snack for Jamaican children.

1 ⅓ CUPS DARK BROWN SUGAR

¼ CUP WATER

3 CUPS FLOUR

1 TEASPOON BAKING POWDER

½ TEASPOON BAKING SODA

½ TEASPOON GROUND GINGER

1 TEASPOON GRATED NUTMEG

2 TABLESPOONS MELTED BUTTER

MAKES ABOUT 2 DOZEN BULLAS Preheat the oven to 400°. Grease a cookie sheet well. Mix the sugar and water together in a bowl until they become a syrup. In another bowl, sift the dry ingredients and add the sugar syrup and melted butter. Mix well and place the dough onto a well-floured surface and pat the dough into ¼-inch thickness. Using a doughnut cutter, or two glasses of different diameters, cut the dough into circles so that the bullas resemble small bagels. Place the bullas on the cookie sheet and bake them for 20 minutes, until golden.

BUN

Bun and cheese is a Jamaican Easter dish that most travelers never taste unless they are in the country around the Easter holidays and invited to someone's home. The bun is a bit like a dark fruitcake, but has fewer dried fruits. It is usually eaten with a cheese that bears a startling resemblance to Velveeta, but it is equally good when paired up with a good sharp Cheddar. This is one case when authenticity is best sacrificed to taste. It is a great snack and an interesting ethnic addition to a tea table.

¼ CUP (½ STICK) BUTTER

¼ CUP (½ STICK) MARGARINE

1 POUND FLOUR

½ TEASPOON BAKING POWDER

1 ⅓ CUPS BROWN SUGAR

½ TEASPOON GRATED NUTMEG

½ CUP CURRANTS

½ CUP RAISINS

½ CUP MIXED DRIED FRUIT PEEL

¼ CUP CHOPPED DRIED CHERRIES

2 EGGS

⅓ CUP MILK

MAKES 1 LOAF   Preheat the oven to 300°. Blend the butter and margarine into the flour in a mixing bowl. Add the baking powder, brown sugar, nutmeg, currants, raisins, dried fruit peel, and cherries and mix well. In a separate bowl, beat the eggs and pour them into the flour and fruit mixture. Slowly add the milk until you have a loose batter. Pour the batter into a greased 10-inch loaf pan. Bake for 1½ hours, until golden. Test for doneness by inserting a knife into the center of the cake. If it comes out clean, the bun is done. Remove, let cool, and serve with Cheddar cheese slices.

BAKES

Bakes are a traditional accompaniment to many Trinidadian stews. They hark back to the time when many Caribbean dishes were one-pot meals and the starch was either a rice, a coocoo mixture, or a quick bread, like bakes. These bakes reflect a new Caribbean health consciousness and are prepared with margarine instead of the more traditional shortenings. Though these are cooked in hot oil, they were traditionally cooked on a flat baking stone.

2 CUPS FLOUR

½ TEASPOON SALT

2 TEASPOONS BAKING POWDER

2 TABLESPOONS MARGARINE

2 TEASPOONS LIGHT BROWN

SUGAR

½ CUP WATER

1 CUP VEGETABLE OIL FOR FRYING

MAKES 2 DOZEN   Sift the dry ingredients into a large bowl. Rub the margarine into the dry ingredients until you have a mixture with a cornmeal-like texture. Dissolve the sugar in the water, add it to the ingredients, and mix until you have a soft dough.

Knead the dough lightly for 5 minutes on a floured surface and cut it into 1½-inch pieces. Heat the oil in a heavy cast-iron pot until it smokes. Then roll the pieces into balls, flatten them until they are about ¼ inch thick, and drop them into the oil a few at a time. Cook for about a minute, or until they are browned. Alternately, bakes can be cooked on a hot griddle. In this case, cook slightly longer, turning to make sure they are browned on both sides.

SWEET CORN BREAD

Most visitors to the Caribbean think of corn bread as a southern black culinary hallmark. Not so. Corn bread and breads made from cornmeal turn up in several Caribbean countries. This sweetened corn bread is a Dominican variation on the more familiar corn bread recipe. It calls for such Caribbean additions as grated coconut, brown sugar, cinnamon, nutmeg, and raisins.

¾ CUP YELLOW CORNMEAL

½ CUP FLOUR

¼ CUP GRATED COCONUT

3 TABLESPOONS DARK BROWN
   SUGAR

3 TEASPOONS BAKING POWDER

¼ TEASPOON SALT

½ CUP MILK

¼ CUP FRESH OR UNSWEETENED
   CANNED COCONUT MILK

1 EGG

3 TABLESPOONS COCONUT OIL

½ TEASPOON GROUND CINNAMON

½ TEASPOON GRATED NUTMEG

¼ CUP DARK RAISINS

MAKES ABOUT 1 DOZEN PIECES   Preheat the oven to 425°. Grease well a 6-inch square baking pan. Place the dry ingredients in a large bowl. Add the remaining ingredients and stir for 2 minutes, or until the mixture is a smooth, thick batter. Pour the batter into the prepared pan and bake for 20 minutes, or until light brown on top. Serve hot with butter.

ROTI

Roti is a traditional accompaniment to southern Caribbean curries. In Trinidad and Tobago, the crepelike roti, filled with a curried potato and chicken mixture, is a favorite street food and almost an alternative national dish. In Guyana, where there is also a sizable Indian population, the roti is dipped in the curry and eaten as an accompaniment. This recipe, from my friend June Bobb, is one Guyanese variation of roti.

2 CUPS UNBLEACHED WHITE FLOUR	¼ TEASPOON SALT
	WATER TO MAKE A STIFF DOUGH
¼ TEASPOON BAKING POWDER	CORN OIL FOR GRILLING

MAKES 4 TO 6 ROTI Sift the dry ingredients into a bowl. Add enough water to make a stiff dough. If you have added too much water, add a bit more flour so that the mixture is stiff. Form the dough into 4 to 6 balls. Flatten each ball with a rolling pin. Spread each roti with corn oil and a bit of flour. Fold the roti back into a ball by turning the ends in on each other. Let the roti stand for at least half an hour. When ready to cook, heat a griddle or a heavy cast-iron skillet. Roll out the roti into flat crepelike forms. Cook until lightly browned, turning frequently, for 3 minutes. Drizzle a small amount of corn oil on the side of the roti that is not cooking, then turn it to keep it from sticking. Remove the roti from the griddle, place it in the palm of your hand and "clap" your hands together 2 or 3 times, taking care not to burn yourself. Serve the roti hot with a chicken curry and homemade chutney.

RUM CAKE

Rum is the alcoholic hallmark of the region, as much a part of the Caribbean's history and everyday life as breathing. It is only natural that Caribbean baking should devise a way of celebrating this. Here it is rum cake, the islands' answer to baba au rhum.

1 CUP UNSALTED BUTTER	2 CUPS FLOUR
1 ½ CUPS LIGHT BROWN SUGAR	½ CUP CORNSTARCH
4 EGGS	2 TEASPOONS BAKING POWDER
JUICE OF 1 LIME	⅓ CUP BARBADOS RUM
¼ TEASPOON GRATED LIME RIND	

MAKES 1 9-INCH LOAF   Preheat the oven to 350°. Grease well a 9-inch loaf pan. In a bowl, cream the butter, gradually add the sugar, and beat until light. Add the eggs one at a time, beating the mixture after each egg. Add the lime juice and rind and stir well. Sift the dry ingredients together and add them to the batter, stirring constantly. Finally, add the rum. Beat well and pour the batter into the prepared pan. Bake for 1¼ hours, or until brown on top and a knife inserted in the center comes out clean. Serve warm with rum raisin ice cream.

BANANA BREAD

When it's teatime in the Caribbean, along with such traditional English delicacies as scones and clotted cream, you're likely to find other treats that speak of their island origins. One such item that has found favor in northern climes is banana bread. Served warm or cool, the bread brings the taste of bananas to the tea table. Banana bread is also surprisingly good toasted and topped with a tropical jam.

¾ CUP WHITE SUGAR	2 CUPS FLOUR
¼ CUP DARK BROWN SUGAR	1 TEASPOON BAKING POWDER
¼ CUP BUTTER	½ TEASPOON BAKING SODA
3 RIPE BANANAS, PEELED AND MASHED	DASH OF VANILLA EXTRACT
	RUM TO TASTE (OPTIONAL)
1 EGG	

MAKES 1 9-INCH LOAF   Preheat the oven to 350°. Grease a 9-inch loaf pan well and line with wax paper. Cream the sugars and butter together in a large mixing bowl. Add the mashed bananas and mix well. Add the egg, the dry ingredients, and the vanilla. You may add the optional rum. Pour the batter into the prepared pan and bake for 50 minutes, or until well browned. A knife inserted into the center of the loaf will come out clean when the bread is done. Remove and allow to cool on a rack for 10 minutes, then serve warm or wrap in foil and freeze.

COCONUT PUDDING

The coconut turns up in almost all guises in Caribbean cooking. It is baked and broiled as appetizers; it finds its way into soup, enriches main and vegetable dishes, and is the backbone of Caribbean confectionery. However, when it comes to baking, the coconut is in its element, turning up as coconut bread and as an ingredient in everything from corn bread to coconut pudding. This coconut pudding is a rich variation on the bread pudding theme. It can be served plain or topped with meringue.

2 CUPS GRATED FRESH OR DRIED
  UNSWEETENED COCONUT

2 CUPS FRESH BREAD CRUMBS

4 EGG YOLKS

1 CUP MILK

1 CUP COCONUT MILK

5 TABLESPOONS BUTTER

6 TABLESPOONS BROWN SUGAR

1 TABLESPOON VANILLA EXTRACT

2 TABLESPOONS MOUNT GAY RUM
  OR OTHER BARBADIAN RUM

SERVES 4 TO 6   Preheat the oven to 350°. While the oven is heating, place all of the ingredients together in a large bowl and stir them until they are well mixed. Then, pour the mixture into a large ovenproof dish. Bake for 1 hour. Serve warm.

SAINT KITTS

PUMPKIN BREAD

Bananas, pineapples, oranges, and even pumpkins all find their way into various Caribbean breads. In this pumpkin bread, you may use either the traditional West Indian cooking pumpkin or calabaza, or the more common U.S. "Halloween" pumpkin. In either case, the bread is simple to make, is delicious served warm, and stores beautifully in the refrigerator or freezer. This is a good recipe for those who like to bake gifts for friends during the holiday season.

3 CUPS SUGAR

1 CUP VEGETABLE OIL

4 EGGS

1 CUP BOILED PUMPKIN MEAT,
    MASHED INTO A PULP

3 CUPS FLOUR

MAKES 2 8-INCH LOAVES   Preheat the oven to 350°. Grease and flour 2 8-inch loaf pans. In a large bowl, mix all of the ingredients together. Stir well and pour into the loaf pans. Bake the bread for 1 hour, or until golden brown. When done, a knife inserted into the center of the loaf will come out clean. Turn the bread out onto a rack and allow to cool for 10 minutes. Serve warm or wrap in foil and freeze.

PINEAPPLE BREAD

Antigua's pineapples, instead of the more traditional bananas, are a major ingredient in this tangy bread. It is an interesting alternative to banana bread at a Caribbean tea.

⅓ CUP BUTTER

⅔ CUP LIGHT BROWN SUGAR

1 EGG

2 CUPS FLOUR

4 TEASPOONS BAKING POWDER

1 TEASPOON SALT

2 CUPS FRESH CRUSHED
    PINEAPPLE

MAKES 1 9-INCH LOAF   Preheat the oven to 350°. Grease well a 9-inch loaf pan. In a large bowl, cream the butter and slowly add the sugar, beating well. Then, add the egg. Sift the dry ingredients and add them to the mixture. Fold in the pineapple and mix well. Place the dough in the prepared pan and bake for 1 hour, or until light golden. The bread is done when a knife inserted in the center comes out clean. Serve warm.

DESSERTS

AND

SWEETS

D-r-r-r-ring!! the little bell goes off as you enter the door as if to signal that you have crossed the threshold into a special place. At La Fontaine Fleurie in Fort-de-France, Martinique, sugar is king, if not emperor. The *confiserie,* or sweet shop, still makes many of the traditional delicacies that delighted colonists. The pristine glass showcases display a seemingly endless variety of candied tropical fruits, *chadec glacé* (candied shaddock rind), and *papaye confit* (candied papaya). There's also crystallized ginger; brown sugar fudges; sweetened fruit pastes prepared from passion fruit, mango, ginger, lime, and the like; coconut patties; and a wide array of coconut and brown sugar–based treats.

La Fontaine Fleurie and similar sweet shops in Guadeloupe do a lively business sending sweets to homesick Antilleans in France and around the world. When they arrive, the intricately wrapped CARE packages bring the expatriates a taste of the tropics and of the culinary delights that used to be.

ADELLA

Christophine is almost always thought of as a vegetable and served either steamed, *au gratin,* or even in fritters. The innovative chefs at Jamaica, Jamaica, a resort on that island's north shore, have come up with a delicious dessert in which the bland squash takes on the tropical flavorings of rum and brown sugar.

1 POUND CHRISTOPHINE SQUASH

   (CHAYOTE)

½ TEASPOON GROUND CINNAMON

1 CUP WATER

1¼ CUPS DARK BROWN SUGAR

6 OUNCES DARK JAMAICAN RUM

6 SCOOPS COCONUT ICE CREAM

SERVES 6   Wash the christophine, peel it, and cut it into bite-size pieces. Place the pieces, ¼ teaspoon of the cinnamon, and the water (or enough to cover) in a saucepan and bring it to a boil. Cook for 5 to 7 minutes, until the christophine is cooked through but still firm.

In a skillet, heat the brown sugar until it liquefies. Add the christophine and the remaining ¼ teaspoon of cinnamon to the brown sugar. Pour in the dark rum, a bit at a time, while stirring the mixture thoroughly. Serve the christophine and the sauce over scoops of coconut ice cream.

BANANES FLAMBÉES

Bananas appear flambéed as dessert in almost all of the countries of the Caribbean. This is Martinique's variation on the classical theme.

¼ CUP GOLDEN RAISINS

¼ CUP FRESHLY SQUEEZED
　ORANGE JUICE

4 RIPE BANANAS

2 TABLESPOONS UNSALTED
　BUTTER

2 TABLESPOONS DARK BROWN
　SUGAR

PINCH OF GRATED NUTMEG

¼ CUP RUM

SERVES 4　　Place the raisins in the orange juice until they expand. Meanwhile, peel the bananas and slice them in half lengthwise. Heat the butter in a large frying pan and add the bananas, round side down. Cook the bananas for 2 to 3 minutes on each side, turning them carefully with a spatula so as not to break them. Mix the sugar and nutmeg with the raisins and juice and pour it over the bananas.

When ready to serve, remove the bananas from the frying pan, reserving the cooking juices, and arrange them on a hot plate. Heat the cooking juices to boiling, add the rum, and light it, pouring it over the bananas. The alcohol will burn off, leaving you with a rummy aftertaste on the sautéed bananas.

BROWN SUGAR FUDGE

Barbados's sugarcane made fortunes for English planters in the eighteenth and early nineteenth centuries. Even today, Barbados is one of the Caribbean islands where cane is an ever-present reality in some areas. Driving through a tall cane field is awe-inspiring. The bamboolike canes tower over you and seem to close in after you. Distances are telescoped, the world fades away, and the cane creates its own universe away from that of reality.

Cane sugar comes in different forms in the Caribbean ranging from new sugar, an almost liquid form, through a seemingly endless color spectrum of browns to the processed sugar that most Americans and Europeans are familiar with. This recipe calls for light brown sugar, but could equally well be prepared with dark brown sugar, which will give the fudge a bit more of a molasses taste.

2 CUPS LIGHT BROWN SUGAR	2 TABLESPOONS UNSALTED
⅔ CUP MILK	BUTTER
2 TABLESPOONS LIGHT CORN	1 TEASPOON VANILLA EXTRACT
SYRUP	1 TABLESPOON RUM
¼ TEASPOON SALT	

MAKES ABOUT 3 DOZEN 1-INCH SQUARES
Butter a 9-inch cake pan. Place the sugar, milk, corn syrup, and salt in a saucepan and cook over medium heat, stirring constantly, until the sugar is dissolved. Continue to cook, stirring occasionally, until the mixture reaches 234° on a candy thermometer, or when a small amount of the mixture forms a soft ball when dropped into very cold water.

Remove the mixture from the heat, stir in the butter, and allow the mixture to cool to 120° without stirring. Add the vanilla and rum and beat well with a wooden spoon, until the candy becomes thick and loses its shine. Spread the mixture in the pan; allow it to cool until it is firm, and then cut into 1-inch squares. The fudge will keep for about 2 weeks in a covered jar in the refrigerator.

TABLETTES DE COCO

Creole candies are, unfortunately, an unheralded form of creole cooking. The candies frequently place the accent on coconut and brown sugar, but the changes are rung in with a variety that is astonishing. Coconut fudges, coconut patties, candied exotic fruits, and more are island delights. These coconut bars are typical of Martinique.

2 CUPS FRESHLY GRATED	1/4 TEASPOON GROUND CINNAMON
COCONUT	1 3/4 CUPS BROWN SUGAR
1 CUP WATER	DASH OF VANILLA EXTRACT

MAKES 1 DOZEN Place the grated coconut in a saucepan with the water and cinnamon and cook over a medium flame for 30 minutes. Add the sugar and vanilla, lower the heat, and simmer, stirring frequently, until you have a very thick, almost crystallized mass. Remove from the heat and form the mixture into bars on a piece of confectioner's marble or a chilled, oiled cookie sheet. These will keep for about 2 weeks in a closed jar in the refrigerator.

ROCHERS CONGOLAIS

The name, which means Congolese rocks, aptly describes the look of these coconut candies. The praline-colored, coconut-filled candies are a traditional Creole sweet and are often found in the fancily wrapped packages from the Creole *confiseries,* like Martinique's La Fontaine Fleurie.

4 EGG WHITES	2 CUPS FRESHLY GRATED
1 HEAPING CUP LIGHT BROWN	COCONUT
SUGAR	1/4 TEASPOON VANILLA EXTRACT

MAKES ABOUT 2½ DOZEN ROCHERS   Place the egg whites and the sugar in the top of a double boiler over a low flame. Whisk constantly until the mixture is frothy and hot. For best results, do not stop whisking until the mixture forms stiff peaks. Remove from the flame and fold in the grated coconut and vanilla.

Heat the oven to 400°. Grease a cookie sheet and drop the rochers onto it by the teaspoonful, pulling slightly so that they look like small pyramids. Bake for about 20 minutes, or until the rochers are golden on the outside and slightly soft in the interior. The candy will keep for 2 weeks in a jar in the refrigerator. (If they last that long!)

TRIFLE

Many a diner has been surprised at the end of a Caribbean meal to find that this classic English dessert has made its way to the region. Trifle is not a recent arrival; mentions of the dessert occur in numerous accounts of plantation life. Recipes for the dish were given as far back as *The Lucayos Cookbook,* which is thought to have been published on Andros in the Bahamas in the late seventeenth century. Here is a more modern variation, which makes a fancy dessert when served in a cut-glass bowl.

ENOUGH STALE POUND CAKE TO
   FILL A MEDIUM-SIZE GLASS
   BOWL
1 CUP PINEAPPLE JAM (PAGE
   114)
¼ CUP DARK BARBADOS RUM

1½ CUPS MILK
2 EGGS
1 TABLESPOON LIGHT BROWN
   SUGAR
CANDIED PINEAPPLE AND OTHER
   FRUIT TO DECORATE

SERVES 6 TO 8   Slice the pound cake, spread it with the pineapple jam, and layer it in the glass bowl. Moisten the cake and jam with the rum and ½ cup of the milk.

Prepare a custard from the remaining cup of milk, eggs, and sugar. Beat the eggs and the sugar lightly. Heat the milk in a small saucepan and add the egg and sugar mixture. Continue to cook over a low flame, stirring constantly, until the eggs thicken. Do not allow the mixture to boil or the eggs will curdle. Allow the custard to cool, then pour it over the cake mixture. Decorate with candied pineapple and other fruit, and serve.

CHADEC GLACÉ

The *chadec* or shaddock (see Glossary) is a lumpy relative of the grapefruit, which is traditionally used for this candied peel. However, since it
is much easier to find grapefruit and the taste is not appreciably different,
I have substituted it. These can be served as after-dinner candies or diced
and added to chutneys, Christmas cakes, and cookies.

3 PINK OR WHITE GRAPEFRUIT   1 ½ CUPS WATER

  SKINS   1 CUP LIGHT BROWN SUGAR

3 CUPS WHITE GRANULATED

  SUGAR

Scrub the grapefruit skins well, remove the membrane and as much of
the white pith as possible. Place the skins in a saucepan, cover with water,
and cook them until they are tender when pricked with a fork. Remove
them, allow them to cool, and cut them into bite-size strips.

    Place the white sugar and 1½ cups water in a second saucepan and
cook, stirring occasionally, until the sugar reaches 325° on a candy thermometer or spins a thread. Drop the grapefruit peels into the syrup and
cook until they are transparent. Shake half of the brown sugar over a cool
surface (marble is best), then remove the peel from the syrup and place it
on the bed of brown sugar. Cover it with the remaining brown sugar and
allow it to dry. The *chadec glacé* (or candied grapefruit rind) will keep for
months in glass jars.

CRYSTALLIZED GINGER

Jamaica's ginger is famous the world over for its taste and its abundance. In fact, the country is occasionally even known as the "Land of Ginger." A dash of the rhizome finds its way into many Caribbean main dishes and into most of the condiments, and powdered (ground) ginger is a frequent ingredient in much of Jamaica's baking. Crystallized ginger is also frequently found and is nibbled on as a digestive after meals.

1 PIECE OF GINGER, ABOUT HAND-
   SIZE
1 ½ CUPS WHITE GRANULATED
   SUGAR

¾ CUP WATER
½ CUP LIGHT BROWN SUGAR

Peel the ginger, removing all of the outside skin and fibrous tough parts, and cut into thin slices. Place the ginger slices into a saucepan, cover with water, and cook until the ginger is tender when pricked with a fork. Remove the ginger and allow it to drain.

Meanwhile, take the water in which the ginger has been cooked and add enough to it to make ¾ cup. Place the water in a saucepan and add the white granulated sugar. Cook the mixture, stirring occasionally, until it reaches 325° on a candy thermometer or spins a thread. Drop the ginger slices into the syrup and cook for 2 to 3 minutes.

Shake half of the brown sugar over a cool surface. (Confectioner's marble is best.) Remove the ginger slices and place them on the marble to cool. Sprinkle them with the remaining brown sugar. These will keep well for weeks in a tightly closed jar in the refrigerator.

SALADE DES FRUITS
TROPICAUX

The cornucopia of tropical fruits that are available in the region provides Caribbean cooks with inspiration for fantastic fresh fruit salads. On Guadeloupe, this inspiration coupled with French culinary influences and a love of good food comes together to produce a variety of fruit salads featuring local fruits such as custard apple, passion fruit, cashew fruit, sapodillas, and more. As these fruits are not readily available in the States, I've limited myself to what can be fairly easily found in this version of an exotic fruit salad. If you live in an area where other fruits are available, use this as a guideline and then experiment.

2 RIPE MANGOES, PEELED AND CUT INTO ½-INCH DICE

2 FIRM RIPE BANANAS, PEELED AND SLICED INTO RONDELS

1 CUP FRESH PINEAPPLE CHUNKS

2 BLOOD ORANGES, SECTIONED

1 STAR FRUIT, SLICED

¼ CUP LIGHT RUM

½ CUP GRATED FRESH COCONUT, TOASTED

SERVES 6 TO 8   Mix all of the fruits together in a medium-size glass bowl. Pour the rum over the fruit, mix it well, and allow the fruit salad to sit for 30 minutes. When ready to serve, sprinkle the toasted coconut over the top of the salad. This salad can be prepared without the rum, but it does lose some of its zing.

MANGO SORBET CHEZ CLARA

Mangoes are the quintessential tropical fruit. They appear on tables as garnishes for meat dishes, in chutneys, and in fruit salads, and are served whole as snacks and as fruit desserts. Some folk (myself among them) are fond of the flavor of mangoes but, much to the disgust of mango aficionados, do not like the fibrous consistency of the fruit. Imagine my delight when I discovered this mango sorbet at Chez Clara's restaurant in Guadeloupe. It retains all of the wonderful tropical sunshine flavor of the mango, without the fibers.

2 CUPS MANGO PULP (ABOUT 5
  MEDIUM MANGOES)
¾ CUP EXTRA-FINE SUGAR
¼ CUP DICED MANGO FOR
  GARNISH

4 SPRIGS FRESH PEPPERMINT FOR
  GARNISH

SERVES 4   Prepare the mango pulp by putting the peeled, pitted mangoes through a food mill to eliminate all of the fibers. Sprinkle with sugar and allow the sugar to dissolve in the mango pulp. Place the pulp and sugar mixture in freezer trays in the freezer compartment of your refrigerator for 3 hours, removing it at 30-minute intervals to beat it with a fork to be sure no ice crystals form. Alternately, you may use an ice cream machine, following the manufacturer's instructions. Serve cold with a sprinkling of diced mango and a few sprigs of mint as garnish.

QUICK TREMBLEQUE

This coconut custard, which adds the New World ingredient of coconut to the classical Spanish dessert, flan, is a traditional dessert in much of Hispanic America. This dish frequently appears on Cuban Lucumi and Puerto Rican Santeria altars as a favorite food of the Yoruba god of purity, Obatala. It was from followers of these religions that I learned the quick method. Quick trembleque, quite simply, cheats.

Take the trembleque packaged by Goya products and enhance it by using coconut milk instead of the regular milk called for in the package directions. Actually, it's one of those cases where you can get away with a bit of step-saving and not disappoint your taste buds.

JAMAICA

MATRIMONY

The romance in this dish comes from its name and from its exotic ingredients, which traditionally include star apple. As this fruit is not readily available in most northern climes, I have substituted an apple-and-pear mixture for it in this variation.

1 RIPE PEAR, PEELED, CORED, AND CUT INTO ½-INCH DICE	2 ORANGES, PEELED AND SECTIONED
1 McINTOSH APPLE, CORED AND CUT INTO ½-INCH DICE	¼ CUP CONDENSED MILK GRATED NUTMEG

SERVES 6   Place the pear and apple dice into a cut glass or crystal bowl. Remove all membranes and seeds from the orange sections and add them to the bowl. Mix the fruit together, sweeten with the condensed milk, and add nutmeg to taste. Then, cover and chill in the refrigerator for at least 1 hour before serving. Serve chilled.

GUAVA CHEESE

This is a traditional dish, served as a dessert along with a bland white cheese in many Spanish-speaking countries. The guava "cheese" is not a cheese at all, but rather an intensely flavored paste made from guava pulp and sugar. Guava cheese is available at stores selling Hispanic products, but it is quite easy to make. As the paste keeps well, you may wish to make it in a larger quantity and store it in a glass container in the refrigerator.

2 CUPS GUAVA PULP (SEE NOTE) (ABOUT 5 MEDIUM GUAVAS)

2 CUPS WHITE GRANULATED SUGAR, PLUS EXTRA FOR COATING

MAKES ABOUT 1 DOZEN 1½-INCH SQUARES
Place the guava pulp and the sugar in a saucepan and bring the mixture to a boil over medium heat. Lower the heat and continue to boil the mixture, stirring constantly, until it takes on a jamlike consistency and begins to shrink from the sides of the saucepan. (The mixture should form a soft ball when placed into a glass of cold water.)

Pour the mixture into a greased flat pan or baking dish. Allow to cool and cut into 1½-inch squares when firm. Toss the squares in white sugar, if desired. Serve either as a sweet or accompanied by cheese in the Spanish manner.

N O T E • *Guava pulp can be prepared by putting peeled ripe guavas through a food mill.*

DUNKANOO

Jamaican ethnologist Leonard Barrett speaks of African roots in Jamaican folk tradition in his seminal work, *The Sun and the Drum*. In one of the book's most moving passages, he describes his trip to Ghana's Koromantyn Market in the shadow of the infamous Koromantyn Castle. It was there thousands of West African slaves departed for the New World, including many Gold Coast natives who would end up in Jamaica. As Barrett recounts the story, he spotted a familiar dish of grated corn mixed with sugar and other ingredients and steamed in a banana leaf and identified it by the name that was familiar to him—dunkanoo. With mounting excitement and amazement, he was told that in Ghana, the dish was known as *dokono* and that the ingredients were virtually the same as those he had known in Jamaica. Here, then, is a recipe for one version of dunkanoo, a dish that has survived slavery.

6 NEARLY DRY EARS OF YELLOW
   CORN ON THE COB

1 CUP DARK BROWN SUGAR

2 CUPS THICK COCONUT MILK

½ CUP DARK RAISINS

2 TEASPOONS GROUND CINNAMON

¼ TEASPOON GROUND GINGER

2 DOZEN 4-X-6-INCH PIECES OF
   BANANA LEAF OR ALUMINUM
   FOIL FOR STEAMING

MAKES ABOUT 2 DOZEN PACKETS   Grate the corn into a medium-size bowl. Add the remaining ingredients, except leaves, and mix into a paste.

Meanwhile, bring a large pot of water to a boil over medium heat. Dip the banana leaf pieces into the boiling water to make them pliable. Place 2 tablespoonsful of the dunkanoo mixture into each banana leaf and tie with string into a small packet. Place the dunkanoo packets into the boiling water and cook over a low flame for 45 minutes. When done, remove the packets, allow to cool, and serve. Let the diners remove the banana leaf and enjoy.

MANGO FOOL

Mangoes are a way of life in the Caribbean, not simply a tropical treat as they are in the United States; schoolchildren swipe them from neighbors' trees. Everyone can recite a veritable litany of types and preferences. Julie mangoes range in color from green to pinkish red and turn up almost everywhere. Imperial mangoes and Peter mangoes are other popular versions. Mangoes turn up in everything from pepper sauces and chutneys to meat marinades. They appear on breakfast tables, in luncheon fruit salads, in baskets as after-dinner treats, and on dessert tables where they may appear as mango fool.

6 RIPE MANGOES

6 TEASPOONS SWEETENED
   CONDENSED MILK

1 CUP LIGHT CREAM

1 TABLESPOON LIGHT BROWN
   SUGAR

1 TEASPOON FRESHLY SQUEEZED
   LIME JUICE

DASH OF GRATED NUTMEG FOR
   GARNISH

SERVES 6 TO 8 Peel the mangoes, remove the pits, and put the mango flesh into a blender. Add the remaining ingredients and blend on high until well mixed. Pour into a serving bowl or individual dishes. Chill and garnish with a grating of nutmeg.

BEVERAGES

Coconut water is everywhere in the Caribbean. When you look up at a coconut tree and see the coconuts hanging there looking so much like an enormous bunch of greenish brown grapes, you're looking at coconut water. An old calypso says:

COCONUT WOMAN IS CALLING OUT,
EVERY DAY YOU CAN HEAR HER SHOUT.
GET YOUR COCONUT WATER.
IT'S GOOD FOR YOUR DAUGHTER.
IT WILL MAKE YOU FEEL TIPSY.
MAKE YOU FEEL LIKE A GYPSY.
IT WILL MAKE YOU FEEL FINE.
MAKE YOU STRONG LIKE A LION.

Many natives and visitors to the Caribbean would nod in hearty agreement with the lyrics. Coconut water, whether slurped or sipped more genteelly from a straw straight from the shell of a chilled coconut, is ambrosial. It is reputed to be a superb morning-after hangover cure as well as a night-before offender in the notorious mixture of rum and coconut water (and therein lies yet another calypso!).

Occasionally you will find green or water coconuts in Caribbean markets. They are also called jelly coconuts in some islands, because the coconut meat is still jellylike. Some enterprising folk here in the States have even set up their own summertime stands, lobbing the tops off chilled green coconuts in the back of vans, in neighborhoods where there are lots of people from the Caribbean. If you find such a stand, get the largest plastic bottle you can, wash it out, and bring it back for a filling with coconut water. You'll be hooked. After you've got the liquid, ask the vendor to open the coconuts so that you can savor the jellylike meat. It's slippery, slidy, and oh, so good.

GREEN COCONUT
WATER

The recipe here is simple; opening the coconut is the problem. If you are handy with a machete, or cutlass as it is called in the English-speaking islands, you're on your own to try your luck at opening one.

1 GREEN COCONUT   1 MACHETE

SERVES 1   Risking all 5 fingers and your career as a concert pianist, whack the top off the green coconut to open a hole. Pour the liquid out into a frosted glass. Savor.

The variations on this theme are endless. Try mixing the coconut water with dark rum or even with gin or vodka for a different type of tropical drink.

The coward's version of this recipe calls for a nearby vendor to do the opening. Please note that the Asian canned coconut water that is available for sale in some Caribbean markets is not the same thing. It has been sweetened.

PIÑA COLADA

The piña colada is one of the classic Caribbean rum drinks. The combination of pineapple, coconut cream, and rum makes what many vacationers think of as a very adult milk shake. The trick is not to get the piña colada too cloyingly sweet. This is best achieved by using real pineapple instead of pineapple juice in mixing the drink.

1 ½ OUNCES WHITE PUERTO
   RICAN RUM

1 OUNCE CREAM OF COCONUT

1 CUP FRESH PINEAPPLE CHUNKS,
   PLUS 1 WEDGE FOR GARNISH

½ CUP CRUSHED ICE

SERVES 1   Combine all the ingredients except garnish in a blender for 15 seconds or so. Serve in a tall chilled glass or a hollowed-out pineapple shell. Garnish with a pineapple wedge.

C U B A

FROZEN MANGO
DAIQUIRI

Legend has it that Papa Hemingway found the daiquiri at La Floridita restaurant in Havana. Others, though, point to the Daiquiri iron mines in Santiago, Cuba, and suggest that the drink was originally invented by mine workers there relaxing after a hard day. The decline of cocktail shakers brought in the invention of the frozen daiquiri and with it any number of flavored daiquiris made with everything from strawberries to pineapple. This frozen daiquiri calls for ripe sliced mango for its tropical taste.

6 OUNCES WHITE PUERTO RICAN
  RUM

1 TABLESPOON FRESH LIME JUICE

2 TABLESPOONS SUPERFINE
  SUGAR

⅓ CUP FRESH MANGO CHUNKS,
  PLUS 3 CHUNKS FOR GARNISH

2 CUPS ICE

SERVES 3   Place all of the ingredients except garnish in a blender and puree until the mixture has the consistency of wet snow. Pour into chilled stemmed cocktail glasses and garnish with a mango chunk speared on a toothpick.

MOJITO

Another one of Papa Hemingway's Cuban hangouts was a small restaurant known as the Bodequita del Medio. The well-known artists' haunt boasts walls that are inscribed with the signatures of all who have visited. Roast suckling pig and black beans and rice are obligatory treats, as are Mojitos, a little-known drink made with rum, soda, and spearmint.

¼ OUNCE FRESHLY SQUEEZED
  LIME JUICE

1 TEASPOON SUPERFINE SUGAR

4 FRESH SPEARMINT LEAVES

2 OUNCES WHITE RUM

2 DASHES OF ANGOSTURA BITTERS

ICE CUBES

CLUB SODA

SERVES 1   Place the lime juice, sugar, and 2 of the spearmint leaves in a chilled tall glass and mix them well, pressing down on the muddler to bruise the mint. Add the rum, bitters, and ice cubes. Top off with soda water and garnish with the remaining 2 mint leaves.

SHANDY

This is a British drink that has been transplanted with ease into the Caribbean. The mixture of beer and ginger beer is a perfect thirst quencher, and the range of Caribbean beers is vast. If you can get a Caribbean beer in your neighborhood, try Jamaica's Red Stripe, Haiti's Prestige, Barbados's Banks, or Trinidad's Carib. If not, use any light lager.

1 12-OUNCE BOTTLE LIGHT LAGER BEER

1 12-OUNCE BOTTLE GINGER BEER

2 DASHES OF ANGOSTURA BITTERS

GRATING OF NUTMEG

SERVES 2 Place 2 glass or pewter beer mugs in the freezer to frost. When frosted, mix half a bottle of beer with half a bottle of ginger beer in each mug. Add a dash of bitters and a grating of nutmeg to each mug. Serve immediately and drink chilled.

SORREL

Sorrel is a red flowering plant that is a member of the Hibiscus family. It comes into bloom around the Christmas holidays and is a traditional Christmas beverage in much of the English-speaking Caribbean. The flowers are mixed with other flavorings to make a dark red aromatic drink, which can be served plain or mixed with rum. Sorrel has become so popular that it is available in northern Caribbean markets virtually year round.

2 HEAPING CUPS DRIED SORREL

3 WHOLE CLOVES

1½ TABLESPOONS GRATED ORANGE ZEST

1½ TABLESPOONS GRATED FRESH GINGER

1 QUART BOILING WATER

1½ CUPS SUPERFINE SUGAR

MAKES 1 QUART   Place the sorrel in a large crock with the cloves, orange zest, and ginger. Cover with boiling water and let it steep for 24 hours.

Strain the sorrel and add the sugar to the mixture, stirring well. Pour the liquid into a sterilized quart bottle that can be loosely stoppered. Add a few grains of uncooked white rice to the bottle. (No one is sure *why* you do this, but it's traditional.) Allow the bottle to stand for 2 days for the mixture to mature, and then serve the sorrel mixed half and half with water. You may want to add a generous dose of Mount Gay or other rum to your glass of sorrel. That's all a part of the Christmas spirit.

LAVENDER TEA

The cane fields of Barbados are overwhelming. In some parts of the island, they surround the road on either side and block views of anything else for miles. Ironically, as Lewis Carroll must have not known much about sugarcane and its disorienting effect on some people, driving through the cane is very much like falling down the rabbit hole. This effect is heightened when at the end of the road you stop at a small colonial house lost in the cane. Here, a small tearoom has been created in the true *Alice in Wonderland* mode: There are pink walls and tables where you might find yourself seated as the guest of Mr. Ted E. Bear or one of his stuffed animal friends. The menu is a combination of British tea and fantasy with a selection of beverages ranging from lapsang soochong to lavender tea.

1 TABLESPOON DRIED LAVENDER   HONEY TO TASTE

SERVES 1   Place the lavender in a 2-cup teapot which you have heated by swishing it out with boiling water. Add boiling water to fill and allow the tea to steep for several minutes. Pour into china teacups and add honey to taste. Serve hot and don't forget to invite Mr. Bear if he's in the neighborhood.

GREAT HOUSE
RUM PUNCH

The traditional Caribbean rum punch recipe is so common that there are even souvenir tea towels and aprons with it emblazoned on the front.

ONE OF SOUR

TWO OF SWEET

THREE OF STRONG

FOUR OF WEAK

It seems that the planters who lived in Jamaica's great houses did not exactly adhere to this recipe. Their punch, which seems closer to the Ti-Punch of Martinique and Guadeloupe (see following recipe), really packed a wallop.

3 OUNCES DARK JAMAICAN RUM	1 TEASPOON HONEY
(APPELTON, MYER'S, WRAY AND	CRUSHED ICE
NEPHEW)	1 TABLESPOON WATER
1 OUNCE FRESHLY SQUEEZED	GRATING OF NUTMEG
LIME JUICE	

SERVES 1   Mix the rum, lime juice, and honey well with a swizzle stick and pour it into a 6-ounce glass that has been filled with crushed ice. Add the water and top with a grating of nutmeg. Serve at once.

TI-PUNCH

Any time is a good time to savor a ti-punch in Martinique or Guadeloupe. When the noon sun beats down on the *savane* in Fort-de-France, Martinique, and you stop for an aperitif before lunch at a café, that's perfect.

When you've had a successful day and want a slight pick-me-up on the way home, that's perfect. When the evening requires some settling into and the guests haven't arrived yet for dinner, that's perfect. When you stop for a few acras and a ti-punch with some friends, that's perfect. Any time is a good time to savor this drink. In Guadeloupe, the cane sugar syrup the recipe calls for will frequently be replaced by small tropical fruits in syrup. You can adjust the sugar syrup to taste.

¼ TABLESPOON CANE SUGAR   1 ICE CUBE

  SYRUP   1 ZEST OF LEMON

1 OUNCE WHITE MARTINIQUEAN

  OR GUADELOUPEAN RUM

SERVES 1   Place the sugar syrup in a small wineglass, add the rum, an ice cube, and the twisted lemon zest.

PUNCH VIEUX

If a ti-punch is a friendly anytime drink, a punch vieux speaks to more weighty matters. This is a drink to be consumed during heated political discussions among friends. Traditionally an evening drink, the punch vieux is well suited for the hour when it is time to begin the beguine and the sky is turning from day to night at what the French call *l'heure bleue*. The punch vieux uses dark rum, occasionally even the *rhums agricoles* that delight rum connoisseurs with their complex cane taste and their molasses nose. For this reason, out of respect for the rum, the lemon zest and ice cube are omitted from the ti-punch recipe. Here, again, the sugar syrup should be adjusted to taste.

¼ TABLESPOON CANE SUGAR   1 OUNCE DARK MARTINIQUAN OR

  SYRUP   GUADELOUPEAN RUM

SERVES 1   Place the sugar syrup in a small wineglass, add the rum, and stir with a swizzle stick. Serve.

MAUBY

Although I have listed mauby as being a Barbadian drink, it is a local beverage in many parts of the Caribbean. Traditionally, mauby is prepared from tree bark, which is infused in water. The liquid is then diluted with more water, flavored with vanilla, and sweetened with sugar. Up until fairly recently, it was not unusual to see vendors in the main streets of Caribbean towns or in marketplaces selling mauby, and virtually every housewife had her special purveyor. Today, things have changed. Mauby is available packaged in supermarkets and even sold in bottled form to be diluted to taste. Since the method of preparation will depend on the type of mauby that you find, I will leave this one up to you. Simply follow the package directions. Then add ice and savor.

CHAMPOLA

This drink is prepared from soursop nectar, vanilla ice cream, and rum. It is a beverage that frequently turns up at religious ceremonies for the African god, Obatala, a member of the Yoruba pantheon who found his way, along with the Yoruba religion, to Cuba and later to Puerto Rico. At religious ceremonies, the drink is prepared without rum for Obatala, a temperate orisha (deity) who does not drink. A traditional story has it that while molding the human beings who were to inhabit the earth, Obatala became drunk on palm wine and created people with deformities. Seeing what he had done, he was ashamed and forever after refused strong drink. You can take your choice: Without rum, the drink is a cooling summer milk shake. With it, it gives the piña colada stiff competition.

1 CAN GOYA SOURSOP NECTAR   4 JIGGERS RUM (OPTIONAL)

2 CUPS VANILLA ICE CREAM

SERVES 4   Place all the ingredients into a blender and blend until smooth. Serve in stemmed glasses.

PIMENTO DRAM

For years I thought the Pimento Dram that I passed in various Jamaican airport shops was an exotic liqueur prepared from bell peppers. I could not imagine how it might taste and was not intrigued enough to consider a purchase. Imagine my surprise when I discovered that Pimento Dram is actually made from allspice berries, known as pimento in Jamaica, and is not only tasty, but easily prepared at home and makes lovely holiday presents.

1 CUP RIPE ALLSPICE BERRIES

2 CUPS FRESHLY SQUEEZED LIME
   JUICE

1 QUART WHITE JAMAICAN RUM

¼ POUND CINNAMON STICKS

2 QUARTS WATER

4 POUNDS GRANULATED SUGAR

MAKES ABOUT 1 GALLON   Place the allspice berries in a crock with the lime juice and rum and let them stand for 3 days. Crack the cinnamon and boil it in the water. Remove the cinnamon sticks and bring the water back to a boil over medium heat. Add the sugar and continue to boil for about 10 minutes to produce a cinnamon sugar syrup.

Meanwhile, remove the allspice berries from the lime juice and rum, add the syrup, and strain the mixture into decanters for gifts, or into quart bottles. Cork and let stand for 2 days and then enjoy.

CARIBBEAN BLOODY MARY

For those of us who like Bloody Marys, it is hard to conceive of the drink made with anything but vodka, and pepper vodka at that. However, when I was recently in Puerto Rico, I took a trip to the Bacardi rum factory where I was introduced to the Rum Bloody Mary. It works. The trick here is that the rum must be Puerto Rican rum because it is so smooth that its taste does not intrude on the tomato juice. Starting with that information, I went on to experiment, using Caribbean ingredients to replace the traditional Tabasco and Worcestershire sauce, and voilà . . . the Caribbean Bloody Mary.

½ CUP TOMATO JUICE

1 JIGGER WHITE PUERTO RICAN
   RUM

JUICE OF ½ LEMON

¼ TEASPOON CELERY SALT

1 TEASPOON PICKAPEPPA SAUCE

½ TEASPOON OR MORE RED DEVIL
   PEPPER SAUCE (PAGE 124)

FRESHLY GROUND BLACK PEPPER
   TO TASTE

2 ICE CUBES

1 SCALLION, INCLUDING 4 INCHES
   OF THE GREEN TOP, FOR
   GARNISH

SERVES 1   Mix all the ingredients well in a cocktail shaker, except the ice and garnish. Pour into a chilled stemmed glass into which you have placed the ice cubes. Add the scallion for garnish. Sip and feel the tropical heat.

BANANA MILK SHAKE

In a country where bananas literally grow on trees and recalcitrant children don't always wish to drink their milk, it is inevitable that someone would come up with a banana milk shake. This one, though, is for adults.

1 CUP MILK

½ RIPE BANANA, PEELED

1 TEASPOON SUPERFINE SUGAR

DASH OF VANILLA EXTRACT

2 OUNCES DARK JAMAICAN RUM

(APPELTON, MYER'S, WRAY AND

NEPHEW)

1 SCOOP VANILLA ICE CREAM

SERVES 2   Place all of the ingredients in a blender and blend. Pour into two 8-ounce glasses and serve immediately.

MAIL ORDER SOURCES

Most of the ingredients needed to prepare the recipes in *Sky Juice and Flying Fish* are readily available; in cases where they are not, substitutions have been suggested. There may be a few, however, that are hard to find in your neck of the woods. My standard answer to questions about obtaining Caribbean ingredients is, "Head for the nearest place that you hear reggae music." When a friend replied, "Oh, you mean my daughter's room . . . ," I realized it's not quite that simple. Many cities, though, do have Caribbean enclaves where calabaza, chiles, and coconuts can be found with no problem. If you know one nearby, it's guaranteed to be the best source. Gourmet food shops may also surprise you with prepared products like Pickapeppa Sauce from Jamaica or Bonney Pepper Sauce from Barbados. Some Caribbean products overlap with Asian or Latin American products and can be found in the appropriate shops. If all of these are unavailable, you may wish to try one of the following mail order sources.

The Creole Marketplace
885–887 Nostrand Ave.
Brooklyn, N.Y. 11225

Delmar Imports
501 Monroe St.
Detroit, Mich. 48226

Aphrodisia Products, Inc.
282 Bleeker St.
New York, N.Y. 10014

Jamail Family
3333 South Rice Ave.
Houston, Tex. 77706

Dean and Deluca
560 Broadway
New York, N.Y. 10012

Pier I Imports
5403 South Rice Ave.
Houston, Tex. 77706

Cardullo's Gourmet Shop
6 Brattle St.
Cambridge, Mass. 02138

The Central Grocery
923 Decatur St.
New Orleans, La. 70116

Also don't miss markets such as:
La Marqueta in New York City, the Central Market in Los Angeles, Pike Place Market in Seattle, and the French Market in New Orleans.

INDEX

LIQUID AND DRY MEASURE EQUIVALENCIES

CUSTOMARY	METRIC
¼ teaspoon	1.25 milliliters
½ teaspoon	2.5 milliliters
1 teaspoon	5 milliliters
1 tablespoon	15 milliliters
1 fluid ounce	30 milliliters
¼ cup	60 milliliters
⅓ cup	80 milliliters
½ cup	.120 milliliters
1 cup	240 milliliters
1 pint (2 cups)	480 milliliters
1 quart (4 cups, 32 ounces)	960 milliliters (.96 liters)
1 gallon (4 quarts)	3.84 liters
1 ounce (by weight)	28 grams
¼ pound (4 ounces)	114 grams
1 pound (16 ounces)	454 grams
2.2 pounds	1 kilogram (1000 grams)

OVEN TEMPERATURE EQUIVALENCIES

DESCRIPTION	°FAHRENHEIT	°CELSIUS
Cool	200	90
Very slow	250	120
Slow	300-325	150-160
Moderately slow	325-350	160-180
Moderate	350-375	180-190
Moderately hot	375-400	190-200
Hot	400-450	200-230
Very hot	450-500	230-260